RUSSIAN JUSTICE
The Horror & The Fear

Memoir by
Valera Minin

First published by Huge Jam Publishing, 2020.

ISBN: 978-1-911249-27-6

My graduation from police college, 1976

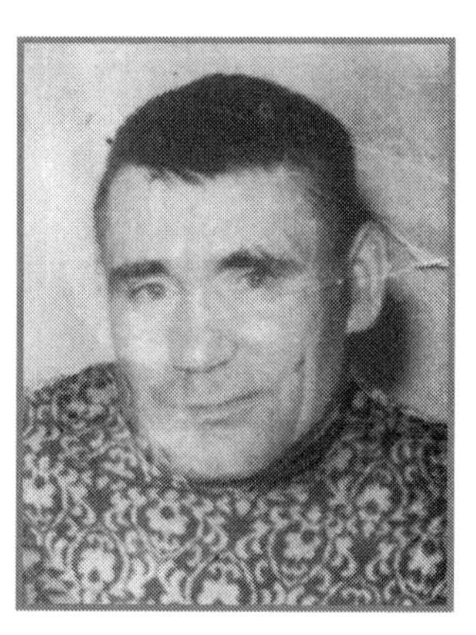

Yevgeny (Eugene) Mezhogsky

This book is dedicated to the heroism
of my father-in-law,

Yevgeny Petrovich Mezhogsky

as well as to my struggle with state criminal
investigators, prosecutors, judges and the betrayals
and deceptions in the totalitarian regime of the
USSR and then Russia.
This is my war against the state.

Valera Minin

Contents

PROLOGUE

This book is the story of my life and my family. As you read it, put yourself in my position and consider: *how would I be feeling and what would I have done?*

This book is also about the so-called 'mysterious Russian soul'. And a complete mystery to me is the manner in which Russians judge non-Russians. Specifically, how they judge the indigenous population of the Komi Republic and render them powerless.

This book is dedicated to the heroism of Yevgeny Petrovich Mezhogsky who fought and defended his country and homeland, through all the horrors of war, was courageous as a Prisoner of War in Osventsem, seeing death every day, every hour, every minute and then giving his life for his most beloved daughter of six

Yevgeny is like the son of God, not composed of the lies that flooded through the veins of Nikolay Komlev, ASSR Investigator of Internal Affairs, who 33 years later took revenge on the participants of the Second World War.

Yevgeny Petrovich is worthy of a posthumous Nobel Peace Prize – at his death he warned of the death of the Soviet Union for which he had fought. The Soviet Union as he liked to remember it, before all the corruption set in. That was the death he meant. In the reborn Russia we do not have the right to have things, alibis vanish, and we give birth to children in prison.

This book is about the fact that we, as Komi ethnic minorities, cannot deny crimes of which we are accused; our confessions will be written for us anyway.

Above all, this book is about misuse of power, lawlessness, corruption, perjury in the enforcement agencies, courts and the CPSU regime throughout the USSR, and a most cynical and heinous crime against that most holy thing: a pregnant woman. My wife and Yevgeny's daughter, Galina Minina...

This book is about the horror of Russian justice.

Valera Minin, Syktyvkar, 2020

1

PART OF THE LANDSCAPE

My name is Valera Minin. Son, husband, father, ex-lieutenant in the Soviet militia, trial witness, defence lawyer, psychiatric prisoner. I have experienced good times and, for the past 40 years, I have experienced the unimaginably painful.

Beyond everything I have experienced the excruciating ache of injustice.

This memoir is a statement to the world that corruption is still alive and kicking in Russia and, oh boy, do I feel kicked!

But I will start from the beginning, before the controversies. This will be from memory; I didn't keep a diary though it sometimes occurred to me that I should. I had no inkling that my life would contain episodes worthy of sharing. In fact, I wasn't really even aware of being me. I was another part of the beautiful Komi landscape, part of my family, part of the typical, happy, mundane world in which we enveloped ourselves. But now I will attempt to individuate myself… And I will first emerge in the village of Rimya on July 7th, 1951.

Looking back at this time, my first thoughts are of nature. The house of my childhood was on the shore of a lake. The views were beautiful. This is often true of any view that features a sea, a lake, a river, or even the tiniest of streams. Beyond the water I could see a beautiful field, with flowers. And behind us? A forest. The air was sweet and clear, though peppered generously with mosquitos.

Rural landscape near Ust-Vymsky, Russia, Komi Republic

My childhood pastimes were my responses to what nature had laid out for us there: for my parents Peter and Maria, and my older brother and sister Alexander and Raisa. With my brother Alexander, three years my senior, I would fish, and I would hunt ducks; especially in autumn when the water became a temporary stopping place for every southward-bound duck, goose and swan, or so it seemed. Modest prey, given that the region of Vorkuta translates as "an abundance of bears!" In the capital of Komi, in the city of Syktyvkar, they do not see this side of nature and therefore cannot understand the passion it invokes!

So far, so idyllic: and that was indeed my young perception. But nature had also provided the Vorkuta region in the Komi republic with an abundance of something much darker: coal. This coal was the foundation for something darker still… one of the Gulag's largest and most notorious forced labour camps.

Mining there started under Stalin's rule in 1932 at the height of the Gulag's[1] power, the coal having been discovered just one year earlier. Georgiy Alexandrovich Chernov received awards for this geological and financial discovery but those people who were repressed and who found themselves illegally condemned, well,

[1]The Gulag was a Soviet government agency in charge of the forced labour camp system. Millions died in these 'gulags'. Lenin introduced it, but Stalin saw to it that the agency was at the height of its power in the 1930s-50s.

they cursed and despised Chernov and Stalin because they were sent to the Taiga, to build a railroad to Vorkuta for mining that precious black stuff. Laying sleepers in minus 50 temperatures, buffeted relentlessly by strong winds. Ten years later, *Vorkutlag* – the largest forced labour camp in European Russia – was connected to the rest of the world via a prisoner-built railway line; the general belief being that the price of the railway's construction was one human life for each sleeper laid.

So it was that my beautiful village was a 'rural locality' situated in the north of the coal-mining Komi ASSR. My mother told me that we occasionally gave food to the Baltic prisoners who were led in columns through our village, carried on river barges. Her heart went out to them. The famous Russian writer Alexander Solzhenitsyn, a famous opponent of the Gulag, later linked the influx of Ukrainian prisoners to the incident to which I now turn…

In 1953, there was an uprising among the camp inmates. After two weeks of a fairly peaceful stand-off the Chief of Camp, Derevyanko, possibly buoyed by his mass arrest of saboteurs on the previous day, ordered guards to open fire on the inmates: nearly fifty were shot dead, and more than a hundred were injured. Further deaths followed as a result of medical help being temporarily withheld (at Derevyanko's request). Our region's first notable brush with corrupt politics.

Can a surname affect the fate of an individual? I believe it can. You will find in Moscow a monument to two men who fought for the liberation of Russia: Kuzma Minin and Dmitry Pozharsky. These heroes created a militia to fight for freedom and liberation in Russia against its Polish invaders. It is to Kuzma Minin that the events of my life are dedicated. I have the same surname Minin and I also fight; but against the enemy within – corruption, lawlessness and the arbitrariness of judges in the USSR and now in Russia.

My father Peter was born in 1905 and spent part of his childhood in the company of the eminent Pitirim Sorokin. Sorokin would have been twenty years old, my father just seven; therefore, I cannot claim that there were any noteworthy political discussions between the two of them! Just lots of fun times crayfish-catching and forest-foraging! My father remembered the time most fondly.

After the October Revolution, Sorokin – anti-communist and a member of the Esser Party – went into hiding after having been arrested several times and even sentenced to death. With Lenin's personal help he escaped execution by travelling to the United States, where he continued to work as a professor of sociology, and supporter of human rights, until he retired from Harvard in 1959.

Sorokin

Most versions of history state that Lenin wanted him arrested, but actually I can tell you now that the opposite is true, and there was a bond of underlying respect between the two men, especially on Vladimir Lenin's side. Lenin mentions Sorokin in every volume of his writings. He admired Sorokin's honesty and integrity: an admiration detailed by his own accounts in each volume of his *Meetings*. You can compare this to the relationship between Stalin and Pasternak, detailed later in this book.

Sorokin had certainly been very honest in much that he wrote about Lenin! I read an article by Sorokin, the title of which says it all: "Lenin. A Fanatic and a Social Extremist." In it, he addresses the reader and asks him or her to:

"Look at Lenin's face. Is it not the face that can be seen in the Lombroso album of born criminals?"

He goes further.

"Lenin is not only a character from the Lombroso album, but also a good teacher of another from that same album: Adolf Hitler."[2]

But now, I wish to return to descriptions of my mother and father...

My father fished his way into adulthood! And it was on board a fishing vessel in Murmansk that he sustained the injury that kept him out of the war... when he lost his fingers to a winch. Not fighting suited his own distinct lack of politics. Not quite so much on a domestic level unfortunately, and I would always side with and protect my mother when I saw his hand raised in anger.

Yes, my father loved to drink, and often cursed my mother and raised his hand. I always stood up for my mother. My brother Alexander was afraid of our father. Maybe this is an early sign of my fearlessness and my attempt to help a person in need. In Russia they say: "If the husband drinks, then half the house burns, and if the wife drinks, then the whole house burns." My mother did not drink.

My mother, Maria Ivanovna, was born under the rule of Tsar Nicholas II in 1910. From an early age she had a devout belief in God and managed to hold on to

---

[2]Current History 1924, Chicago Press

her faith and live by it for all of her 94 years. Her wisdom and intelligence belied the fact that she had received only three years of schooling. Despite (or perhaps because of) her longevity, she was always very pragmatic about the fleeting nature of life. I remember once asking her about how fast life seemed. She said that time did indeed go very quickly, but that was just the way it was.

My instinctive memories of her are flavoured with food and milk… but not just for infantile reasons! Yes – she fed me very well: Mother loved to cook with her traditional Russian stove, the treasured stove that imparted at least as much taste into the food as it did aroma into the house. There is nothing like a Russian stove! It is not only a good way of cooking (there is nothing better), but the stove also gives warmth to the house. You can sleep on the stove, and also watch the fire burning there. I would wake in the morning to the warm smell of *koloboks*[3]. But my mother was also a milkmaid on the collective. She worked hard on the farm and more often than not harvested the biggest milk yields. If I could not find my mum at home, then I knew she was hard at work with the dairy herd.

---

[3]Kolobok is also a character in Russia's national fairytale. The equivalent of 'The Gingerbread Man'.

Koloboks and milk

A traditional Russian stove

My mother retired when I was 14. Looking back at a 1965 copy of our regional newspaper *Vperyad* [*Forward*], I saw an article about Maria Minina being the farm's hardest-working woman and how she had received a party and a gift-bestrewn 'send-off' at her retirement. "Is this right?" was my question to her. She shook her head and I felt keenly, and for the first time, the hypocrisy of casual propaganda, the lies of the Soviet press and embezzlement of money from the state: my mother's bosses wrote out the expenses for her retirement banquet and then drank it themselves. She was even lied to about her pension, receiving two times less than the amount promised to her. A shortfall in income that troubled her greatly. She felt hurt by her treatment and insulted by the meagre pension.

That feeling of injustice moved from her to me, like a spark, as I reread the misleading article. It continues to burn in me with more intensity each time a new breath of propaganda whips up the flames. I could have no idea at that young age that my anger over the misleading article about my mother was a faint foreshadowing of the pain I would feel years later upon reading an article about my wife.

2

KALASHNIKOVS AND VODKA

As I moved from my teens to my twenties I was to be found in the army. Between 1970 and 1972 I was a serving electrician, based at the Moscow Border School's shooting range where captured weapons were stockpiled.

Time spent investigating and comparing the various mechanisms of German guns convinced me that the Kalashnikov machine gun was an improved version of a German weapon.

Kalashnikov, who saw a steam locomotive for the first time when he was eighteen years old, had built a machine gun by the age of 21. But the idea of locking in the propellant powder gases was a German one.

During this time my mind was hungry for facts and

learning. I'm probably one of the only people from the USSR who spent his or her spare time in evening classes!

Different generations of the Kalashnikov rifle

I enjoyed studying. There was, after all, very little cerebral exercise in the soviet army. As a small boy I had loved to read, and that passion for words and learning stayed with me.

I also spent a lot of time playing chess with an off-duty mess officer. We would play for butter rations: 20g of butter and three slices of white bread. This was actually a more dangerous gamble for me than for him… if I lost, he took my ration, but if I won then he would still keep his but just give me extra. He always had excess.

The army food generally was harmful to everyone's health, right up to the black bread that induced heartburn. Everything tasted either sour or bitter. A far cry from my mother's cooking with milk and cream.

With open access to bread and butter rations it was no wonder that all army cooks had fat faces. My chess rival was no exception in this regard. His pudgy face developed a long-suffering expression as he tired of me winning and that particular leisure activity proved short-lived in the end.

I didn't exactly ingratiate myself with other comrades either at times. I recall a group of us being sent to clear an area of forest. We lit a fire there and, shortly after, one of our number announced that he had found a mortar bomb. He was champing at the bit to throw it, but I tried to harness his passion for drama by explaining that there was a fair chance it would explode. They tend to do that. It's their thing. I reported the incident to an officer, but my auguring was met with a cold reception. Never mind that we could all have died.

WWII mortar shell

After the army and various false starts on 'Civvy Street' in terms of college choices, I was directed by a friend of my brother to enrol in the police. I managed to do this in the Kirov region. The Komi Republic police rejected me on medical grounds, but it was pretty clear to me that the only thing that was 'unfit' about me was that I was indigenous Komi and therefore judged to be too ready to follow laws and procedures. They are good psychologists, they realised that I would not serve them as they wanted. Prejudice and Irony, an odd yet popular double-act. Let's see how they play out on the Minin billboard…

Although I didn't obtain my Red Diploma[4], due to getting a pig of a grade from just one teacher, Svinin, I excelled at study and especially enjoyed legal science and lateral thinking.

During my training at the militia training college in Kaliningrad, I lived in barracks that overlooked the city. Even then, among the students there were those who accepted bribes and used the money to get rich and rent superior accommodation along with the students from the Caucasus. Those who had entered training already looking forward to the bribes that would boost their earnings.

After graduating, I worked for a while as a criminal

---

[4]Blue and Red Diplomas are certificates of Higher Education. A Red Diploma is equivalent to an Honours degree.

investigation inspector in Kirov's Oparino district centre while my friend from Kaliningrad, Gennady, worked in Kirov as a police officer. I have several stories about Gennady. He had his own brush with the soviet courts when a woman filed a paternity lawsuit against him, and even though he swore the child was not his he ended up giving 25% of his salary each month towards his upbringing. He wasn't happy and started drinking. I will return to Gennady, with a pinch of salt, in a later chapter. It was my first experience of court too, as I went with him for moral support.

But despite my good job, my heart was tied to the Komi Republic. I didn't really understand the pull of native places, but there it was. So, I moved to the village of Zheshart, five kilometres from Rimya.

I didn't get accommodation in the police station and so I lived in an abandoned old house belonging to a good friend, Alexander. It was 1977 and I was about to meet Galina, my future wife.

Comrade Alexander's house was situated 100 metres from the village store called *Prodmag*. In this store worked a beautiful woman: 23 years old, fair-haired, well-dressed, intelligent and full of life. Galina, or Galya. I gave her poems that I'd written, and many bunches of flowers.

Even then the shop that she worked in was over 100 years old. It was cold and very poorly equipped. Her sister-in-law, Tamara, worked there and was due to go on maternity leave. She really had to persuade Galina to take over from her, as I later found out. Now it is demolished, and a brick post office stands in its stead.

There were three of us in our courtship! Me, Galya and an *Izh Planet* motorcycle. In those days it was a common dream to own a motorbike. There were no cars, and motorbikes were in short supply. We both loved the sound of the engine and the freedom of the open road. I would even ride my motorcycle in temperatures of minus 40 degrees, such was the thrill. Coddled, flush-faced, determined bikers were a common winter sight in the Komi Republic of the 1970s. In spring 1978, a certain Inspector Komlev who you will soon come to know as something of an integral cog in our sad story, caught sight of me on my motorbike and later fabricated that it was bought with embezzled money.

In the summer of 1977, I introduced my girlfriend to my mother. My mother, who was without education, then said in the Komi language, "if only there were no problems in the store!" Galina knew the Komi language but said nothing. There was something rather ominous and even psychic about my mother's sense that the shop wasn't all that it could be! Intuition and wisdom combined. I didn't see it at all. But then, I only saw Galina!

Professionally I was still working as a police officer. I didn't have much of a team around me. I suppose I'd have been more impressed with them if I'd been a vodka-drinker too, and my boss would have been more impressed with me if I'd kept him topped up with bottles of vodka like my colleagues did. Instead, he made sure it was always me who worked the holiday periods.

Avoiding confronting crime while embracing their bottles, my team hated the crime-fighting aspect of their 'calling', being mainly fearful and fawning.

The police station where I worked

Galina told me that there was a stock-taking exercise in the store and that she would be busy for three days assisting with it.

I pictured her each day in the whimsical, tiny shop, where everything looked somehow crooked, arriving early to heat up the stove so that the fingers flicking through the receipts and other files could stay as warm as possible. Afterwards, she told me that everything was fine, and I felt happy for her. I believed her.

Why would I not have believed her? I still re-run our conversation and can find no answer to that question.

I was, therefore, happy. I was in seventh heaven. I was in love, and keen to be married. Galya's family had the appearance of good upstanding but modest people, and to all general intents and purposes so they were. The parents liked to drink, but not heavily so, and there were also four brothers and one sister – of her brother Oleg and his wife Tamara, the aforementioned relative who had worked at *Prodmag No. 2* until her maternity leave, I will say much more later. Galya's father, Yevgeny, hunted and fished and would rise at four each morning to go to work. I asked him for the hand and heart of his daughter, and he agreed.

The donation, from Galina's work, of a 1.5 x 2m^2 carpet, worth 150 rubles, warned me that my hopes of a quiet ceremony and nothing more were to be thwarted! (The *Prodmag* colleagues subsequently asked us to contribute back 50% of the price of this 'gift', a fact that Galina hid from me!)

The carpet promised – or from my point of view

threatened! – an evening of drinking and celebration. In terms of guests, I may as well have been an orphan all my life as, wishing to get the day over with quickly, I hadn't invited anyone; but Galina had her whole family there, including her brothers' wives, and ten friends from work.

'we went by bus to register the marriage'

Naturally I had to ask for a day off from my police chief, Danilov. He asked who I was getting married to and I said that she was the daughter of Yevgeny Mezhogsky. Danilov said he knew him and that he was a good man. But I didn't invite him to the wedding; he was always drinking at someone else's expense. In the 1990s, he was killed in an accident; a car had been unable to brake in time as the drunken chief swayed in the middle of the road. He left behind a daughter with special educational needs, who he had conceived in an equally drunken stupor.

I believed both then and now that happiness does not depend on the number of glasses downed. The wedding was basic, we did not celebrate in the restaurant, but celebrated in an old panel-framed apartment building. And we went by ordinary bus to register the marriage. I just wanted my wedding day to be over. My wife seemed a little sad, and I was concerned that she doubted my love for her. I assumed it was me. Little did I know at that point that the die had been cast and that she saw me that day as her policeman-saviour. That surprise was saved for me until the summer of 1978.

Our wedding day was August 25th, 1977. Exactly 362 days later, my wife's work gave us another gift, something that was to shatter more than one life. At our wedding, the taunts of Tamara and her husband Oleg, Galya's brother, had been clues that I hadn't attempted to solve.

3

SCAPEGOATS

Just before my wedding, I got sick.

Three months after the wedding, both Galya and I were in hospital. That hospital stay was the background to the accusation that changed everything.

I live with prostatitis, that has the unfortunate effect of making me prone to extreme sickness with any infection. My condition actually stems from infancy: my mother was given no leave from the collective farm when she gave birth and I had no nanny for much of the time. The -40° frosts were severe, and long-lasting. I developed an infection of the urinogenital system and never fully recovered.

This is just a personal feeling, but it is based on observation and experience: the misdiagnosis and useless medication that I received from a cruel health assistant just before being hospitalised was symptomatic of a great change in the spirit and kindness of the Russian people post-revolution.

People were perverted by the revolution and it turned out that any power to be seized was grabbed by those who had never wanted to work in the first place: alcoholics, criminals, parasites. The revolution was a shock that took millions of victims.

Before the revolution, people believed each other's words and stayed true. Word was bond. Before the revolution, there wasn't even the need to lock up when you left your house, you just put a stick against the door as a sign that no one was in.

But by 1970 those carefree days were long gone, and everywhere were people who would rather do you harm than good.

Just this year, my local newspaper wrote an article about this very nurse who, not content with harming my own health, took revenge upon the health of my son six years later. Yet the report was glowing. Aged ninety now, this woman has received – in the years either side of mistreating me in the 1970s – the *Certificate of Honour of the Ministry of Health of the Komi Republic* "For good work in providing medical care" and the *Certificate of Honour of the Presidium of the Komi Regional Council of Trade Unions* "For fruitful work within the health authority and active participation in public life." The article also celebrated that she had received no fewer than seven greetings cards from a certain Vladimir Putin.

In January 1978, thanks to the timely intervention of the wonderful doctor Suslov Veniamin Mikhailovich, I found myself on the road to recovery. He told me that I was okay and that I needed to relax. He also predicted that I would have my son. But anyway, I digress!

Back to November 1977 when my three-month-old marriage took a turn for the worst... with news from Galina that set in motion the wheels that were to lead to injustice and incarceration... and the death of a good man.

We were both in Syktyvkar hospital, on different floors: Galya was to spend ten days in bed on the floor above my ward. The reason for her admission was a mystery to me, but I knew that gynaecological issues were not always apparent and I also recalled how, before we married, she had mentioned how she didn't want children, and also that she hadn't taken a holiday for three years despite it being a state requirement that everybody take an annual vacation.

While she was at Syktyvkar, others in the little Zheshart shop became suspicious (or rather, as you will see, feigned suspicion) that she had disappeared without warning – and their mock concern was compounded by the fact that we were both 'away' at the same time.

I was still as unaware of the trouble brewing at Galina's place of work as I was of the reasons for her presence in the hospital. But not for long.

Shortly after my wife returned to work as a matter of urgency to heat up the stove – the sub-zero temperatures had caused damage to the food, including shattering glass jars – I received a telegram from her that read quite simply, "Valera come quickly".

*

I was back at home that very evening. Galina, in floods of tears, was almost unrecognisable. "Valera, it was not my fault. Believe me, please! They are using me. I am betrayed. I don't know what's happening! You have to help me."

You can imagine my alarm. As I looked into the eyes of the woman I loved, her innocence and her genuine confusion were more than apparent, as they would have been to anyone even without my emotional commitment. But of what was my wife accused?

The stock-taking I mentioned earlier had highlighted a discrepancy in the accounts, and Galina's sudden and prolonged absence had given her guilty colleagues an opportunity to find a scapegoat.

She had not trusted me originally with the fact that the audit had highlighted a deficit in the takings and so, as I equate trust with love, my conclusion that evening was that Galya did not truly love me. Nevertheless, I wanted to support her. It crossed my mind only later (we grow cynical with age) that she might have fixated upon marrying a police officer in the hope that she would walk free quickly, without the stress of any interrogation.

What follows is the situation in its full complexity… it is not the most interesting part of my story, but it has to be understood!

After three hours of me asking Galina about the store's policies and procedures, her work, various documents, it was clear to me what had happened. She had been deceived over a long period of time by her more experienced and better-educated colleagues: Tamara Yarosh, Tamara Minina, the director Valentina Psurtseva, and the unforgiving accountant, Leonid Yachmenev, who had long harboured resentment against everyone and everything because of his disability.

Procedures at *Prodmag* had been changed under Psurtseva (a new director) and Galina had been left confused by a different way of doing things and by having added responsibility that she had not been trained for. She had entered the workforce after minimal schooling… and her induction was (I would suggest deliberately) limited.

Before stocks were sent on to two other *Prodmag* stores run by Tamara Yarosh and Tamara Minina (there were five stores in all), they were first *all* delivered to Galina in Zheshart, at *Prodmag No. 2.* A new procedure. Due to a busy period with lots of demand from customers, Galina had sent the goods to the respective shops but had forgotten to create and send the relevant invoices. The others had realised this and instead of supporting her with the paperwork, or even just letting her know her error, they had exploited it as an opportunity for fraud.

How were they able to take money from their own stores and not have this reflected in the audit? Tamara Yarosh had bribed Yachmenev, the accountant, to conduct an audit that would clear her, Tamara Minina and Valentina Psurtseva from having stolen any of the 22,000 missing rubles.

To the extent that these three were in communication, we can refer to what was happening in the chain of shops as a conspiracy.

Their backgrounds, and their work responsibilities, I will now list for each.

Tamara Minina was a saleswoman who liked a drink. She worked alongside **Maria Prokopyeva** in the *Prodmag* off-licence store. Galina told me eventually that Minina had deceived her on her return from hospital by getting her to sign an invoice for goods to the value of ₽20,000. More of that later. As a result of the audit, this store was found to have an unaccounted-for shortage of ₽12,000, but neither Minina nor Prokopieva was questioned about this in court. There was a rumour that Minina had bribed Inspector Komlev (who you will see took over the initial investigation) with ₽3000.

Tamara Yarosh was from the Volgoda region and a very experienced crook. Fraudsters do tend to tour the country, moving from place to place leaving a trail of some level of financial destruction behind them. With her three children she had moved to the Vorkuta region in the hope of meeting a rich miner.

But the miners are wise people!

Instead she met and married Andrey Yarosh who was serving a prison sentence. Together they moved to the village of Neftebaza, ten kilometres from Zheshart. Her *Prodmag* store sold household items and food.

Valentina Psurtseva, the boss, came originally from what was then known as the Kazakh Autonomous Soviet Socialist Republic (now Kazakhstan – literally ‘country of wanderers’) and had lived in the city of Sergeevka. There she was involved in crime. Vurdov, a friend of mine who worked in the police, showed me a case file that Inspector Komlev had requested which showed Psurtseva's crimes and the fact that she had been arrested. She had bribed her way out of custody and moved 3000 kilometres to the Komi Republic. She had also been sacked from various director's roles and had changed jobs many times. When she was dying alone, heaps of iron coins were found in her sliding wardrobes – she was so greedy. The coins had depreciated in value!

They must have thanked their lucky stars when Galya and I 'disappeared' to hospital: the word on the street had been that we were taking a holiday with the missing money on an *Izh Planet* motorcycle that had been bought in the same way as the fictitious holiday. Remember the mention of Inspector Komlev's sighting of me on the bike? The accusations got worse as the investigation proceeded.

4

THE DYSHLO

Still smarting inside that Galya had hidden the findings of the audit from me, for fear that I should think her guilty, I determined how best I could help her. "Tell the truth!" I told her. "Say it how it was!" Stupid advice, it turned out! I should rather have told her to take to the bottle, to offer bribes, and to neither remember nor say anything.

So, in the end, we both showed our stupid sides. And in my other side that night, as sleep eluded me entirely, I could feel a metaphorical stabbing from the wife that didn't love me enough to trust me. Looking back, reflecting on her actions and her words, I see now that Galina probably hated me. I wasn't liked enough by my colleagues to be the knight in shining armour she needed. I wasn't part of the court's *Round drinking Table*. But I don't blame her for feeling that way. I discovered that her own family had not been one hundred percent affectionate – one might even refer to some of them as dysfunctional – and it's difficult to recreate something you have never had. Her mother Nadezhda was rather flighty and even unfaithful and did not make life easy for Galina's father. Remember that proverb "A husband drinks and half a house is on fire; a wife drinks and a whole house is on fire"? In this case, this is suitable for the Mezhogsky family. There were no open demonstrations of love and there were periods where the children were moved into care. But I do not judge her mother. I'm sure the stress was a result of her husband's captivity in Germany and Russia during the war.

A few days after the receipt of the telegram, my discharge from hospital, and the unravelling of a closeness I thought I had, Galina was summoned to a meeting by the shop's management. Not just her, but the workers from the other shop branches too. Also present was the inspector of the OBKHSS (anti-fraud squad), Alexey Bersenev.

Standing there all together, we were solemnly given the official notification about the missing money. Within a second of the statement, Tamara Yarosh had fainted like a seasoned fraudster. Many of those present, especially Bersenev, ran around like headless chickens looking for heart tablets! I commented loudly that she was a swindler and that she was simply acting. She was on her feet again shortly afterwards.

Yarosh, like Psurtseva, had clearly moved to Vorkuta with the idea to continue engaging in the kinds of crimes they had both bribed their way out of in their hometowns.

After offering bribes, these two quietly left the meeting. Later, when I looked in the case files, I could see no mention of this event or its outcome. Neither was there any reference to the fact that criminal charges had been brought against the two women before.

*

Unlike for others in post-revolution communist Russia, the 25th day of December in 1977 wasn't 'just another day'. At seven o'clock in the morning, Alexey Bersenev and his two witnesses entered our marital home to seize our belongings.

This house belonged to Galina's grandmother Anna as did the contents. So, for these reasons (as well as for the pure injustice of it) I refused to sign his paperwork.

I knew Bersenev as I had worked with him in the police force: I disliked the man intensely. I had the acquaintance of someone who would regularly tell people how Bersenev had taken him to a large warehouse and encouraged him to join him in taking lots of stuff for free. (A few years after the trial, Bersenev left the area in a *Moskvich-412* car bought with bribes and with a whole railway carriage full of things: building materials, boards, plywood... he was later charged with accepting bribes.) Anyway, this pillar of the community wrote down in his notes that I had refused to sign the house contents, our grandmother's belongings, over to him. He promised us that he would tell the court that the belongings were not ours, but he reneged on this promise as you will see later in the court notes.

One month into the investigation there were complaints about Bersenev because initial investigations are time-limited by law to *ten days only*, therefore the case against us was handed over to a detective from the Investigative Department of the Ministry of Internal Affairs: Inspector Nikolay Komlev.

For the sake of an entertaining narrative I'd like to say something unexpected about this man. But the pattern is established. You don't rise to the top in Russia by doing things fairly. Komlev was about fifty years old and a quiet alcoholic. He always had a bottle of vodka in his case and drank it with small but regular sips. He was from the Kostroma region, born in 1926. Komlev had not fought in the war, but began his career in the NKVD[5] and in his soul he had a deep hatred for the participants in the war.

Although he had a wife and children in Syktyvkar, he spent the duration of the investigation living with 'another' woman, Nefedova, an accountant. She had won his illicit companionship when he 'rescued her' from the threat of fifteen years in prison for stealing ₽50,000 in 1972. He could defend criminals really well. It turned out he wasn't so great at investigating innocent citizens.

It was while walking to this woman's house that he saw me on my motorbike and decided I must have stolen it with *Prodmag* money. He introduced it into the court proceedings and the indictment even though no one ever questioned me about it or even othered to find out the make. Too close to home, Nefedova (and therefore Komlev) lived in the same street as Galya's parents, just 150 metres away from them.

Komlev was told by Danilov that he could do what he liked with me and Galya. I wasn't 'one of theirs' as far as the militia was concerned.

At around the same time as this investigation into Galya's situation, the wife of Vordova, a colleague of mine, was caught stealing an expensive coat – but the

[5]The People's Commissariat for Internal Affairs

case was dropped because she was married to a police officer. As I said, Galina could feel justified in her sore disappointment with me. I was an outsider.

*

Yes, it's true, I was an outsider. But I was still working. In fact, in that same month, December 1977, I was asked to interview a witness to a local murder: the murder of Labytsin by a man named Chebrovsky.

The three men had been drinking heavily all evening in Chebrovsky's house when an argument broke out between the host and the victim. The host raised a hunting rifle to shoot, that he had brought into the room from the corridor. The witnesses pointed out to me that he had then taken the rifle from the room. Although his legs were weak through disability, his arms were big and strong.

Soon after the tension seemed to have been dispelled, Chebrovsky returned unnoticed to the corridor, took up a second hunting rifle and, from his doorway position, fired two shots: one of which hit his stove, the other of which hit Labytsin and killed him stone dead.

Where is this narrative leading, you ask? Well, Chebrovsky's son-in-law turned out to be a member of the Communist Party and the CPSU[6] secretary at the local plywood factory (where Galina's siblings worked). He was able to agree that Chebrovsky be charged with manslaughter rather than murder, despite the statements I had accrued that detailed a premeditated shooting incident. Thanks to his communist connections, Chebrovsky avoided imprisonment and punishment. Relatives of CPSU members can commit crime with impunity. These explanations about the murder remained with me.

There is a saying in Russia, that the 'pole' can turn left or right. It means that the law can apply to individuals in whichever way best suits the judge, and it is usually connected to an individual's politics or wealth. In Russian, the pole is the *dyshlo* – the shaft attached to the front axle of a horse-drawn farm wagon.

Harnessed to the *dyshlo*, the two horses can turn the cart right around. This worldly wisdom entered everyday Russian life from ancient times. Peasants who tried to sue landowners very soon realised that judges applied laws to benefit the rich.

There is another saying in Russia: "honesty is worse than stealing." Galya hadn't stolen anything. There was nothing, not one word, that she could say in court that could have given the judge, Strugovshchikov, or the

---

[6]Russian acronym for the Communist Party

state prosecutor, Plesovsky, any satisfaction or vindication, and that *was* worse for her than if she had been guilty.

So, on February 1st, 1978, we were both of us fired. A coincidence that it was the same day? Galya from the store and me from the police force in a certification procedure connected to bringing the next of kin into criminal liability. Komlev put a massive amount of pressure on Galya, by then in the early stages of pregnancy with our son, to admit under oath to wrongdoing. She was hospitalised twice with the threat of miscarriage during his interrogations. She succumbed to his pressure eventually and his interrogation of her ended. I told her not to fret; *the court, the main court, it will understand, the court trial will reveal the truth.*

Unfortunately, there was a member of our family who from the beginning found such optimism impossible.

5

YEVGENY

Yevgeny Petrovich Mezhogskywas Galina's father. I liked him a great deal. He wasn't perfect, I have already mentioned that the family had issues, but in him I found a great deal to admire.

He was born on July 14th in 1923, six years after the revolution. Like my brother and I, from childhood he had grown to love hunting and fishing – so much so that he would recount with amusement how often he would truant from school, running into the woods to hunt, to a wonderful place where a gun or a catapult was more use to him than a pencil.

At age 19 on 18th April 1942, he was drafted into the army, passed the gunners' course, and was sent straight to the tank division to defend Leningrad under the command of Govorov, Marshal of the Soviet Union.

Almost immediately, not far from the centre of the great city, Mezhogsky was captured by German forces and spent time being transferred between many of the Nazi camps, including Osventz and Zakhausen.

I think the only reason that he survived was that he was so thin and wiry! Slender, but solid. Those days out of school, walking ten kilometres at a time through the forest on his own hunting expeditions, expeditions that continued into his adolescence – right up until the war – yes, those days had served his body well. Yevgeny was a survivor.

It was only when he had indulged in some drinking that my father-in-law would open up about his wartime experiences. He would describe the vicious Nazi beatings he endured each time that he escaped from camp (three times in all), escaping only to be recaptured each time. He would discuss the interrogations he faced from the Germans who could not quite let go of the fact that he had a vaguely Jewish appearance. *I am indigenous Komi*, he would tell them, but still their suspicions, invidious residue of bigotry and brainwashing, lingered and resurfaced. Several times I saw the scars on his back from the lashings he had received during his imprisonment in Nazi Poland.

His ordeals were not even over when he was finally liberated by soviet troops in 1945. All soviet prisoners of war, who by definition had at some point surrendered to the enemy, were cause for suspicion. Stalin ordered his soldiers, the NKVD, to interrogate them regarding any potential treachery. Galya's father was transported to the city of Chrysostom in the Chelyabinsk region. More brutality and mind games. But he passed their tests.

It was in that region, in the city of Zlatoust, that Yevgeny met my mother-in-law, Nadezhda, and fell in love. Though he promised he would take her to live in Leningrad, he brought her instead rather disingenuously to raise a family in the Komi Republic. He loved children and was keen to have a large family. He did not allow his wife to have abortions. Together they had six children: Oleg, Nikolay, Galina, Tatyana, Alexander and Valera. This is the last photograph taken of the two of them together.

Yevgeny and Nadezhda Mezoghny with grandaughter, 1977

Whereas her five siblings were slow to help and reluctant to work, Galya worked tirelessly to support both her parents. When her mother went out and left the children with Yevgeny, as she all too often did – even overnight – it was Galina who would support her dad and reassure him. Not just emotionally but with all the practicalities of running a modest village home: cooking, cleaning, caring for siblings and so on. Her dad meanwhile would be the one who got up every morning at 4am to flood the stove and complete the heavy chores; it was he who made sure the family were never without meat and fish. The two of them were very close; you could say they made a great team.

So, when Komlev called the two parents in for questioning regarding the missing money, his world fell in around him. The Galya he had raised was not a criminal – and yet this was how his daughter was suddenly presented to him by the unflinching and unfeeling inspector. His Galya was a homely child, with no extravagant ways. She didn't even have a winter coat: instead of furs she walked around in a modest spring coat all year round. She neither drank nor smoked. Yet here was this high-ranking police official telling him that his daughter stole and could not avoid prison.

Komlev went further in his attempts to ruin the Mezhogskys. He made a note of their belongings as though they were bought with stolen money, and he presented Yevgeny to the authorities, as well as to the family, as an habitual and heavy drinker, who would have lacked the means to get as drunk as he did *with his own money*. He had (Komlev's developing narrative told) forced his own daughter into crime in order to buy food for the family, while his own meagre earnings only served to support his degenerate lifestyle. Komlev told stories of how Yevgeny was a frequent visitor to the police 'rehab cell', a room set aside for hopeless drunks. Slander is king in Russia.

In defence of my father-in-law, I provided evidence from the police records, a signed certificate, that stated that he had never once been locked up for drunken behaviour.

But this was the last straw for him.

Ladies and gentlemen, a round of applause please for Comrade Komlev who, on July 13th, 1978, finally succeeded where Stalin's inquisition and the Nazi prison camps had failed: Yevgeny Mezhogsky was dead. The Komi hunter, confused, shamed and broken-hearted, aimed his own hunting rifle at his head and fired it on his 55th birthday: one month before Galina's trial came to court. He left a suicide note, but this was hidden away by his wife Nadezhda and Galya's sister Tatyana.

I will let my father-in-law have the last words in this chapter. This is his memoir as recorded by his oldest son Oleg for the *Forward* newspaper in May 2013:

FOR ME, THE WAR BEGAN on the day when my father, Peter Ivanovich Mezhogsky, was taken to the front. From the first days of the war he was on the front line. After being wounded in the leg, he came home on vacation, then again to the front. Peter Ivanovich died in April 1945 in Poland.

I was drafted into the army a little later than my father. My service began in besieged Leningrad as a driving school cadet. The conditions were terrible - hunger, cold, corpses of people who died on the streets, bombing, shelling, fires.

The next place I was in the war was the Leningrad Front, a tank unit, a position – a tanker-machine-gunner of the 220th Tank Brigade. Commander of the front: Lieutenant-General Leonid Aleksandrovich Govorov. My task in the crew was simple – to destroy the enemy's manpower with machine-gun fire. Shooting from a machine gun when a tank rushes at high speed, diving up and down on the potholes, left and right, when the driver manoeuvres, it required a lot of skill. It wasn't shooting in a calm environment at the shooting range. I had acquired a useful skill during the hunt. From my childhood I was wont to disappear in the forest with a gun, hunting for upland and waterfowl, and beating birds into the air. And in combat conditions, when death at every step looks you in the face, there is no choice – either him, or you. The explosions of shells, the bodies of dead enemies and compatriots – an everyday spectacle in battle, a terrible picture, which it is impossible to get used to.

But luck once turned away from us. The tank was hit. The injured crew members, including me, were captured. Three times we escaped but were recaptured by the Nazis. After returning to the concentration camp, we were beaten half to death, they poured water over us and beat us again...

Do not forget Sachsenhausen – a triangular-shaped concentration camp in Germany: towers, barbed wire under voltage, barracks, four crematoriums, gallows, a shooting bay, a shooting room, a gas chamber. If any of the prisoners escaped, the others were not allowed to disperse, they waited for the fugitives to be caught. Three checks were held every day.

On one of the buildings, the camp commandant, walking along the line, stopped near me and, holding out his hand, said: "Yuda!?" I was taken aback – did I, a Komi-Zyryanin, look like a Jew? I looked like all the prisoners of war: sunken cheeks, hollow eyes. Apparently, the fascist noticed my black hair. It was not my plan to burn in the crematorium there and then, and with my thoughts racing frantically I said the first thing that occurred to me: "Chukchi! Reindeer!", emphasising with those words how far away I was from the Jewish nation. A ferocious SS man brought a huge fist down on my head. From the blow, I flew sideways.

When I awoke, I thought: "It seems I escaped the furnace." Then there was Hamburg – again work, unbearable, hard work...

Then – the release, the sending home, first quarantined in the city of Zlatoust, working at a metallurgical plant. For participation in the war, I was awarded the "For Courage" medal and other awards.

I began civilian life. And that is another story...

6

THE TRIAL STARTS

I almost resent Mezhogsky for not being there to support his daughter at her trial. But I must remember that he died an entirely broken man.

The trial began as scheduled, and I wonder now why we all spent so much emotional energy on such a farce. It was 'the hope', of course. Even when I can see the journey something is taking, and the corruption and ineptitude of the men and women at the helm, it is my human nature always to have hope. I think, possibly, I have yet to learn how to manage my expectations even now. For a time then, in that fraught and emotionally charged courthouse, Galina's freedom seemed all to play for…

The date was Thursday, August 17th, 1978. The near-empty courthouse was in the village of Aikino, about 30 kilometres from Zheshart. It is no longer standing but examples of its type are still to be seen across the region: a blue timber building with rows of long white windows. Add a veranda and swing seat and you would have something akin to a New England ranch.

A building similar to the courthouse in Aikino

The simplicity inside was austere and utilitarian rather than modest. I remember, from within its walls, its long, regimented windows – like the inverse of bars on a prison cell wall – proceeding down both sides of the simple rectangular room. A perfect place for the novice art student to practice painting in perspective, placing his or her crucial vanishing point on the other side of the back wall, where we'd all have much preferred to be!

The judge was Yuri Strugovshchikov. About one week before the start of the trial he had shown his bias by sending Galina a letter asking her to repay the shortage, as her payment could then be taken as a mitigating circumstance. Her guilt had not been established and so his request was illegal. He was accompanied by two further 'peoples judges': Orlova and Isakova. The prosecutor was Alexey Plesovsky.

A word about these people who were to judge my wife. Unhappy people have a skewed view of the world's proceedings. I guess the same accusation could now be levelled by the reader at me: but in truth I am an optimist, besides which it was not between the palms of my two hands that power over others was being slowly juggled.

The two female judges were in their fifties. Isakova had no children and resented the presence of my pregnant wife with an omnipresent glowering hatred. Orlova was no happier. Her husband was a heavy drinker who was to take his own life in 1980. During the entire trial there was only one verbal contribution from these women: when Orlova asked Galina how she would send the shop takings to the management. Galina explained that she would fill out a paying-in slip and post it, with the money, to *Prodmag*'s bank account.

Plesovsky (my direct opponent, since it was me who was defending Galina against the prosecution) was a drinking friend of Judge Strugovshchikov. Plesovsky in particular was a heavy drinker who was thrown out of his home by his wife only to drink himself to death by 1996.

How he could have been expected to read out the indictment that day – 15 pages of A4 – with a hangover, I have no idea. Maybe through deep breathing and steadfast determination. Predictably enough, in the end the indictment wasn't read out at all. It would have taken far too long.

In the dock along with Galina were Tamara Yarosh, Tamara Minina, Maria Prokopyeva and Leonid Yachmenev, all of whom had no defence counsel, apart from Galina who had me.

Yachmenev was protected by his membership of the CPSU. He was the main culprit in all of this! He was not even kicked out of the party when they were tried, because organisations have a need for such people: as an accountant he was able to confuse, disguise and delay things. He deliberately concealed the crime but was only tried for negligence. He was on twice Galina's salary and had no wife or children.

Tamara Minina had already bribed the judge. She turned up to court in a fur coat! Her own store had 'lost'

12000 roubles, but she was not questioned about that. Despite it being three times the amount of Galina's shortage.

Prokopyeva claimed that she did not work enough hours to be held accountable for anything, and she was helped by the fact that she was a good friend of Chebrovsky's son-in-law.

Yarosh, in her turn, relied on being the mother of three children who needed her at home.

Also in the courthouse for the indictment was the court secretary, Alla Nesterenko.

At the very start of the trial I petitioned that the proceedings be tape recorded, but the motion was rejected. This actually shattered my spirits from the start, as audio recordings would have made me feel much more confident. I had also requested an additional preliminary investigation as too much had been assumed with no evidence, while the misdemeanours of others had not been investigated at all. Komlev had it and us all stitched up. But my request was again refused. I feel that my performance at the trial was compromised as a result of these refusals and that in other circumstances I might have achieved more for my wife.

Bearing in mind this lack of confidence, one might question why I was her defence counsel. All I can say is 'needs must!' Ten to fourteen days before the start of the trial we had approached a lawyer who, we were assured, had an excellent reputation. A woman called Eta Vikhliaeva. Not only did she express her lack of willingness to be involved, she did so with an unwarranted amount of nastiness, leading us to assume the prosecution had already warned her to step back. A few years later Vikhliaeva's son was killed, hanged with his own tie by someone taking revenge against his corrupt mother for an alleged wrongful conviction.

We had no luck elsewhere either: lawyers claimed that they had been told they could not join court proceedings once they were underway, but that has never been the case. The trouble is that in Russia the prosecutors and lawyers are always, or others might say 'almost always', friends with the judges. Drinks are drunk. Bribes are shared.

So, there I was, very emotionally involved, often fighting back tears, with my only advice to Galina being 'to tell the truth', trusting the simple truth as a scaffold upon which to hang her answers and my questions.

*

The process that day, setting up the framework for the ensuing trial, lasted approximately one hour. The identity of each defendant was established. I added only the information that Galina was pregnant and had already had two miscarriage scares as a result of Komlev's heavy-handed interrogation.

Absent from the courthouse were Galina's siblings. No doubt they were ashamed, and of course we were all still dealing with the suicide of their father. Years later Kolya, the oldest, stated that he'd not known of the trial (which was a lie).

Library photo of a similar courtroom

Oleg, who was also the husband of Tamara – the one who had laughed and sneered at our wedding – admitted 35 years later that he and his wife had known that Valentina Psurtseva was a crook when they had fixed Galya up with the job there. I messaged him while writing this chapter, and you can see his reply to me in the next chapter.

The following day, still in Aikino, the judge asked Galya if she pleaded guilty. I remember the exchange word for word after 40 years! She replied:

"I admit that I discovered and hid the existence of a balance deficit, but I did not steal 1500 roubles."

"But what happened to the 1500 roubles?"

"Probably someone released the goods and forgot to note it."

"So, you embezzled it" declared Judge Strugovshchikov, noting this down immediately as her plea. "You did not steal it, but *you are admitting* to the crime of embezzlement." At this moment, when Strugovshchikov deceived Galina I realised that this was a hoax and my inner voice told me shout "What? are you lying?" But I didn't shout. There were only criminals around, and I understood that.

This was written down as a confession on her part! She did not even understand the definition. So it was that Galina was deceived again, during a process that should have been unbiased.

Unfounded claims continued to be presented as facts: that Galina had been working as the manager of *Prodmag No.2* from January 1976 to December 1977 for the sole purpose of systematically concealing money shortages not just in her own store but in the two others managed by Yarosh and Minina. That, together with them, she had processed the fake invoices that were listed in the indictment and received from, and released to, Yarosh and Minina as un-invoiced goods.

Another deception that the uneducated Galina could not understand featured from the beginning too. Strugovshchikov wrote of missing money totalling ₽4601.54. A shortage that was uncovered by the audit in January 1978. ₽1500 of it was deemed to be the result of wastage from goods transferred by Galina from her shop, while the rest was linked to a collective abuse of official positions. Already charged with stealing ₽4601.54, why would Galina have stolen ₽1500 from herself and incur criminal liability for it? Why was there no further investigation when it would have been clear to anyone in finance that ₽1500 was an arbitrarily-chosen amount with which to smear the wife of an unpopular Komi police officer?

Judge Strugovshchikov

Strugovshchikov had the type of face that expresses very little emotion or personality. A bureaucratic face. The face of inflexibility. The round, uninteresting face that offered his legal spectators a pair of fixed straight lips, a wide pudgy nose, and thin eyes which were later rendered more physically inconsequential still by the addition of a pair of heavy-framed glasses. Small eyes for the small print. Looking at photos now, I see that even the passing decades failed to change his face much. His dark hair went grey, that was all.

I wanted to scream out loud against his deceptions. But what would be the point in a room that housed only criminals? It seemed so wrong that a judge could, with a few carefully selected words, record a slanderous comment at the start of proceedings. It is incomprehensible to me even now. Later, when I researched justice as a concept, I read how even the communist Dimitrov was cleared in a German court of an arson attack on the Reichstag in 1933 due to a lack of evidence. It seemed to me then that only in a Russian court could a judge record a guilty plea, when the defendant had declared the opposite. A German court, in the build-up to the second world war, was fairer than a communist court in 1978.

7

FORGERY

Before I continue with an analysis of the ensuing days at the courthouse, I want to tie up loose ends. Prior to that original stock-taking at *Prodmag*, and around the same time that Galina was given the extra shop responsibilities, Psurtseva had successfully nominated Galina for the position of Zheshart Deputy. This was so that Galina would be overloaded with work and short of time.

Deputies in the Soviet Union equate most closely to town or parish councillors in the UK in the sense that they are responsible for solving local problems; but they are more important politically – almost like remote, or satellite, MPs. There are deputies at local (Zheshart), regional (Ust Vymsky), national (Komi), and federal level (State Duma and Federation Council). Galina's nomination at local level came as a surprise, but I saw later that it was to keep my wife as busy as possible!

With a similar motivation, she made Galina work Sundays and have a day off on Monday so that she was able to speak with her colleagues as little as possible. Then, suddenly, on the Mondays that there was a delivery Psurtseva would summon her in.

Guess what! Deputies are exempt from prosecution, unless an emergency meeting of fellow deputies is called at which they all agree that the accused deputy should be tried. Had Psurtseva 'shot herself in the foot' with this short-sighted attempt to overload Galina so that she didn't notice the fake transactions?

It could have been so… after all, no such meeting of deputies was ever held. Therefore, it actually *should* have been so! But unfortunately for Galina, this was a legal technicality that was voided by the fact that 'someone' arranged for documents to be forged stating that Galina was ejected from her role as a deputy before the start of the trial.

This was never so.

The forged document, which you can compare with the genuine signatures of the same man (Meisner, chair of the session 9th January 1978) on other documents below, was not called into question by the judges or the police and Galina's trial was therefore considered legal.

Years later, our son Vladimir told me to get hold of the documents and check them. I should have done so before but hadn't. That was my fault.

I had great difficulty obtaining access to the files from the *Prodmag* trial. Strugovshchikov would never listen to me nor agree to their release. He saw me as a nuisance. Either that or he was worried that the papers would not stand up to close scrutiny.

Having eventually accessed the files, in particular for this chapter those papers relating to Galina's alleged removal from the post of deputy, I saw the evidence of the interviews with other deputies in which they had *all* of them stated that they had no memory of her removal from that office.

The forged signature that is reproduced below is from the actual 'Withdrawal of Parliamentary Immunity' that is stored in the court files.

Поселковый Совет Р Е Ш И Л :
1. Освободить от депутатских обязанносте
округа №26 тов.Межогских Галину Евгеньев

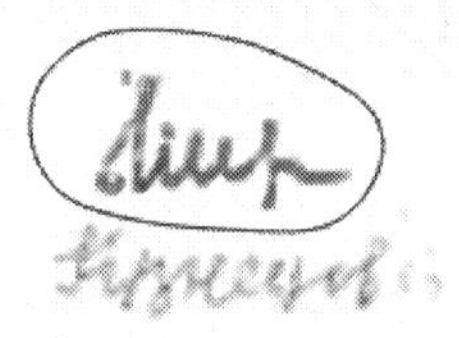

Председатель сессии-
Секретарь сессии-

Vladimir and I were lent the late Meisner's party membership cards by his surviving sons, all of which showed that his signature did not vary for the whole of the thirty-year period to which we had access. The exception being the forged 'withdrawal of immunity' document. We appealed to the investigating authorities, asking them to verify the signature, but they refused on the grounds that Meisner had since died and could not be questioned. It sounds silly, but such are the investigating authorities in Russia. I mean, in that case how is anyone to challenge inheritance disagreements?!

On the following two pages we have the same man's Party membership cards from 1997 and 1973. (Given the fact that Meisner was born in 1918 and that in 1997 he was 80 years old the signatures vary a little. But compare them with the forged signature on the previous page.)

ПАРТИЙНЫЙ БИЛЕТ

№ 04403024

Фамилия Мейснер

Имя Александр

Отчество Карлович

Год рождения 1918

Время вступления в партию ноябрь 1957 г.

Наименование партийного органа, выдавшего билет

Усть-Вымский РК КПСС

Коми АССР

(Личная подпись)

Секретарь партийного комитета

Дата выдачи 10 июня 1973 г.

УПЛАТА ЧЛЕНСКИХ ВЗНОСОВ

1973 год

Месяц	Месячный заработок	Сумма взноса	Подпись секретаря
Январь			
Февраль			
Март			
Апрель			
Май			
Июнь	342	10-26	Мейснер
Июль	350	10-50	Мейснер
Август	364	10-92	Мейснер
Сентябрь	156	2-34	[illegible]
Октябрь	249	4-98	Мейснер
Ноябрь	195	2-93	Мейснер
Декабрь	195	2-93	Мейснер

ПАРТИЙНЫЙ БИЛЕТ

№ 0054378

Фамилия Мейснер

Имя Александр

Отчество Карлович

Год рождения 1918

Время вступления в партию ноябрь 1957г.

Наименование партийного органа, выдавшего билет Усть-Вымский райком КПРФ Республика Коми

(личная подпись)

Секретарь партийного комитета

Дата выдачи 22 апреля 19[illegible] г.

УПЛАТА ЧЛЕНСКИХ ВЗНОСОВ

.... год		.... год	
Месяц	Отметка об оплате	Месяц	Отметка об оплате
Январь		Январь	
Февраль		Февраль	
Март		Март	
Апрель		Апрель	
Май		Май	
Июнь		Июнь	
Июль		Июль	
Август		Август	
Сентябрь		Сентябрь	
Октябрь		Октябрь	
Ноябрь		Ноябрь	
Декабрь		Декабрь	

ZHESHARTT COMMUNITY COUNCIL OF PEOPLE'S DEPUTIES

SOLUTION # 35

January 9, 1978

n. Zheshart

On the release from deputies. AUTHORITIES of the deputy of the electoral district No. 26 of Mezhogskikh Galina Evgenievna.

On the basis of Article 10 of the Law on the Status of a Deputy, in connection with the personal statement of the deputy of the electoral district No. 26 of Mezhogskikh Galina Evgenievna about the addition of deputy powers to her due to circumstances preventing their implementation, the complex audit of all stores of the Zheshart Trade Association was found to have short supply The materials of the criminal case are in the Ministry of Internal Affairs of the Republic.

Village Council R E 'W. AND L:

1. *Release from deputy duties of the deputy of the electoral district № 26 comrade. Mezhogskih Galina Evgenievna.*

Finally, you are waiting to see what Oleg told me about Galina, the shop, and the trial in his online message to me. He continued to deceive us.

> We warned Galya and advised her to quit for a while, while Tamara was on maternity leave, persistently advised her, but she was adamant, I knew Galya's mild nature… We would have come to the court but did not know when the trial was taking place, … but everything ended well, to your great merit, and God punished Psurtseva severely… God sees everything and will not leave offended people in trouble.

He could have visited at any time to find out when the trial was. No helping hand was extended at all. He and Tamara, his wife, did not suggest to Galya that she leave the job: they set her up with it in the first place. Tamara was an employee there and due to leave to have her baby. Another brother, Kolya, was a communist and a deputy, but he too hid like a coward. The pages that follow demonstrate that Justice was as elusive as Oleg and Kolya during the period of Galina's trial.

8

THE STALINIST WAY

Four years was the predetermined sentence that my wife would receive, should she be found guilty of the theft of 1500 rubles. There was no evidence, obviously – how could there be? And in three months she was due to give birth to a baby, our little Vladimir. She stood in front of the judges with downcast eyes in a cream-coloured skirt and blouse typical of the time. She did not spend money on clothes or make-up. Her face was beautiful but showed her stress. She barely raised her head.

She knew that I was the only person who could keep her from four years of imprisonment and, despite my pretence of confidence as I faced the court with my own eyes adopting a challenging stare, she would not have been consoled by my presence. This photograph of Galya and I shows our contrasting characters. Look at our eyes!

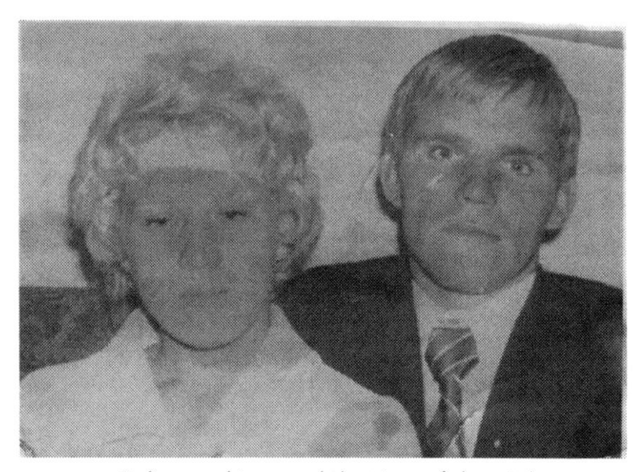

Galina and I around the time of the trial

The court had taken a break for the weekend during which time I had gone alone to Aikino to find the defence lawyer Nikolay Siroklin who was a retired military officer. The judge's deception in making Galina plead guilty to embezzlement on the Friday had shocked me and made me feel out of my depth. Siroklin said that he would find out the details and let me know.

On Monday morning he told me that as the proceedings were already underway, he could not join the process. This was a lie and I suspect that he had been warned off in the same way that Vikhliaeva and others had been. He knew about the trial and therefore had had access to the classified information: he must therefore have met with Strugovshchikov and Plesovsky.

So, on that Monday, 21st August my task began in earnest. My first attempt at questioning was directed towards the prosecution witness Anna Moskotelnikova who was the nearest neighbour of the Mezhogsky family. During the investigation she had told Plesovsky and his team that Galina (and her sister, Tatiana) had been very busy buying furniture, clothes and shoes.

I asked her to name or describe specifically the items that she had seen them buy. She said nothing. She could not perjure herself. She should have been arrested for giving false testimony but, since the court is criminal, she was on the right side. Shortly afterwards (and for an unrelated crime) her own son, not yet married, was sent to prison. He was repeatedly convicted, turned to alcohol, and ended up spending his life locked up.

That same day Tamara Minina came into court. She was obviously drunk, though I did not raise the matter.

I had questions to ask of Galina's mother, Nadezhda, who had already been given a warning by the court for refusing to testify and for giving what they considered to be knowingly false testimony. I asked her what items of significance she and Yevgeny had bought between 1975 and 1977, to which she replied that they had bought nothing and that they had never owned a motorcycle. I asked these questions because of allegations by the prosecution that a whole list of expensive luxury items had been bought by the Mezhogsky family during those three years:

> ...the embezzlement of state property by spending 1,500 rubles' worth of commodities entrusted to her, which is proved by the fact that in the period from 1975 to 1977 the Mezhogi family of which Minina Galina is a member acquired expensive items like a three-winged *Kak* wardrobe, a VEF-2 radio, a carpet 1.5x2m in size, a TV, a sideboard, a *Kazanka* motorboat, a *Whirlwind* washing machine, a *Ural No.3* motorcycle and other things.
>
> Qualification action Minin G., under Art. Art. 170 ch.2 and 175 of the Criminal Code of the RSFSR is correct because Minin G., abusing her official position against the interests of the service out of mercenary motives and a lack of interest by hiding a shortage, caused state interests, namely, Ust-Vymsky district, damages to the amount of 22,505 rubles; - besides this, she committed an official forgery for mercenary purposes in order to conceal the shortage in her store, as well as in the wine-vodka shop and in the shop of "everyday goods" by issuing counterfeit documents, invoices and applying them to the shops' inventory reports.

This was in fact one of the two conflicting motives that Komlev had already listed in his indictment of Galina. I say 'conflicting' because... it is bizarre to claim on the one hand that the Mezhogsky family had been acquiring a host of luxury items with embezzled money while – on the other hand – (the second motive he fabricated) struggling to make ends meet due to the father's drinking habit, to the extent that they allegedly relied on their daughter to steal for them! Neither hypothesis had any truth to it. Even though there were no witnesses, Galina's testimony about how she bought things during those three years that she was working in the store was not presented. This was a fabrication in the style of a Stalinist tyrant. I already mentioned in an earlier chapter that I took police evidence to show Komlev that Yevgeny had never been held in a cell for drunkenness –as the prosecution was claiming. But that wasn't going to worry the accusers or the judges.

There were many other inconsistencies and mistakes on the part of the judge and the prosecution. You might already have spotted the anomaly of the year '1975' being repeatedly mentioned. Galina stood accused of stealing from January 1976, yet the prosecution was falsely accusing the family of having bought items with illegal money in 1975.

Two more things to point out about this: if this claim was levelled against the family, why was Galina the only Mezhogsky in the dock? Where were the other testimonies? Second, many of the items (at least those that existed, such as the wardrobe) had been bought well before 1975 – five, ten, 15 years before *Prodmag No.2* came to feature in their daughter's life! In fact, everything the family owned was inexpensive and entirely commensurate with their monthly income.

And… as we know already… the motorcycle that had been noted was very much mine! I had bought it in April 1977 from the commander of the military unit, Valera Serednyakov, for 250 rubles, not yet knowing Galina.

Nothing that my mother-in-law said was refuted by the prosecution. They let everything she said about their belongings and income stand uncontested. However, *the entirety of Nadezhda's testimony*, prompted by my questions to her, was disregarded in the court protocol and the subsequent sentencing. In other words, *there is no record of any of my questions or of her witness statements in any of the court papers.* It was the Stalinist way. She might as well have been invisible or mute. And how to fight the criminal regime of the CPSU in the USSR?

In addition, Galina's mother and sister both testified that she really did pay for the food she bought for the family. (Komlev, for many months, lied about Galina not having the right to buy products in *Prodmag No. 2*, and needing to go to another store. This was a lie that he tried to coerce her with and this was not the case with the other defendants.)

9

COURT RECORD

Another important witness who should have poured at least a little water on the prosecution's fire had the courtroom been an honest one was a *Prodmag* delivery driver, Mr A Minin. In 1990 he apologised to Galina for his testimony in relation to *Prodmag* logistics. He knew that he was going to die soon and would be receiving treatment at the hospital where Galina worked, and still works, as a nurse.

First there was the following testimony from Psurtseva, taken from page twelve of the court records:

> The witness Psurtseva explained in court that the reports from all those staff who were materially responsible for the import/export of goods were given to Yachmenev. He checked all the documents and, as a rule, always reported

> that everything was in order. The reports were then signed by Psurtseva and she would take them to be stored in Aikino. It was impossible for her to see that the defendants were concealing shortages by inventing consignments.

In this testimony, Psurtseva has correctly demonstrated that goods should only go in one direction: from Galina's central store. The fact that invoices showed that goods were criss-crossing the regions between the shops in both directions is evidence that there was fraudulent activity and attempts to conceal problems. It was at this point that Plesovsky pointed at Psurtseva and said that *she* should be in the dock too.

The driver confirmed in court that, during her time as store manager, he had repeatedly complained to Tamara Yarosh about being asked to make frequent transfers from one store to another against the terms of his contract.

I have quoted from various pages of the court records. The following three pages are facsimiles of the pages I have in front of me right now, followed by their translation into English.

Дело № I-218/78 165

ПРИГОВОР
Именем РСФСР

Усть-Вымский райнарсуд Коми АССР в составе:
председательствующего – Струговщикова П.Л.
нарзаседателей – Исаковой М.Е., Орловой В.Н.
при секретаре – Нестеренко А.В.
с участием прокурора – Плесовского А.М.
и адвоката – Минина В.П.

рассмотрел в открытом судебном заседании в пос. Жешарт 22 августа 1978 года дело по обвинению:

✓ МИНИНОЙ ГАЛИНЫ ЕВГЕНЬЕВНЫ, 7 июня 1954 года рождения, уроженки пос. Жешарт Усть-Вымского района Коми АССР, коми, б/п, образование средне-специальное, замужней, работавшей на Жешартском фанерном комбинате, проживавшей в пос. Жешарт ул. Первомайская 21, ранее не судимой, в преступлении предусмотренном ст. 92ч2, 170ч2 и 175 УК РСФСР

✓ ЯРОШ ТАМАРЫ АЛЕКСАНДРОВНЫ, 21 января 1941 года рождения, уроженки дер. Ситьково Велико-Устюгского р-на Вологодской обл., русской, б/п, образование 7 кл., замужней, имевшей на иждевении трех несовершеннолетних детей, работавшей в Казлукском отделении совхоза "Гамский", проживавшей в пос. Заручейный Усть-Вымского района Коми АССР, ранее не судимой, в преступлении, предусмотренном ст.ст. 92ч3, 170ч2 и 175 УК РСФСР,

✓ МИНИНОЙ ТАМАРЫ НИКОЛАЕВНЫ, 11 августа 1953 года рождения, уроженки пос. Жешарт Усть-Вымского района Коми АССР, коми, б/п, образование средне-специальное, незамужней, работавшей на Жешартской лесоперевалочной базе, проживавшей в пос. Жешарт ул. Бабушкина 11, ранее не судимой, в преступлении, предусмотренном ст.ст. 170ч2 и 175 УК РСФСР

✓ ПРОКОПЬЕВОЙ МАРИИ НИКОЛАЕВНЫ, 22 марта 1956 года рождения, уроженки пос. Жешарт Усть-Вымского района Коми АССР, коми, б/п, образование среднее, замужней, имевшей на иждевении одного несовершеннолетнего ребенка, работавшей на Жешартской лесоперевалочной базе, проживавшей в пос. Жешарт ул. Бабушкина 8, ранее не судимой, в преступлении, предусмотренном ст.ч. 172, 175 УК РСФСР

✓ ЯЧМЕНЕВА ЛЕОНИДА НИКОЛАЕВИЧА, 3 марта 1942 года рождения, уроженца пос. Жешарт Усть-Вымского района Коми АССР, коми, чл. КПСС, образование средне-специальное, холостого, инвалида 3 группы, временно не работавшего по болезни, проживавшего в пос. Жешарт по ул. Центральная 116, ранее не судимого, в преступлении, предусмотренном ст.ст. 172 УК РСФСР, суд

УСТАНОВИЛ:

Минина Г.Е., Ярош, Минина Т.Н., Прокопьева и Ячменев совершили преступление при следующих обстоятельствах:

Минина Г.Е. работая заведующей продовольственного магазина №2 Жешартского Торгового предприятия Усть-Вымского райпотребсоюза, расположенного в пос. Жешарт, с января 1976 года по декабрь 1977 года систематически расхищала вверенные ей товаро-материальные ценности и денежные средства путем растраты.

Допрошенная в судебном заседании Минина Галина виновной себя признала и пояснила, что действительно работая заведующей продмагом №2 с января 1976 года по декабрь 1977 года систематически с целью сокрытия недостачи у себя в магазине а также в магазине у Ярош и Мининой Т. совместно с ними оформляла бестоварные накладные, перечисленные в обвинительном заключении, а также отпускала Ярош, Мининой Т. и получала от них товары без оформления накладных. При передаче магазина продмаг №2 в январе 1978 года у нее была выявлена недостача в сумме 40601 руб. 55 коп. из которых 1900 руб. есть результат растраты вверенных ей товарно-материальных ценностей и денежных средств из продмага №2, остальная сумма недостачи возникла путем злоупотребления служебным положением. Она не согласна с суммой иска в 40601 руб. 55 коп. поскольку при составлении бестоварных накладных совместно с Ярош и Мининой Т. получалась разница, которую Ярош и Минина Т. ей не возместили.

Ярош, допрошенная в судебн...

кументов по приходу и расходу.

Пользуясь этим заведующие магазинами "Продукты №2" – Минина Г., "Товары повседневного спроса" Ярош Т.А., "Вино-водочные изделия" – Минина Т.Н. оформляли бестоварные накладные на якобы отпущенные товары в другой магазин, а также завозили товары без оформления накладных и таким образом скрывали недостачи материальных ценностей, все возраставшие в связи с хищениями ими товаров и денежных средств и злоупотреблением служебным положением.

Таким способом при проведении инвентаризации Ичинеевым были скрыты недостачи, которые причинили существенный вред Усть-Вымскому райпо на сумму 22.505 руб.

Допрошенная в судебном заседании Минина Галина виновной себя признала и пояснила, что действительно работая заведующей продмагом №2 с января 1976 года по декабрь 1977 года систематически с целью сокрытия недостачи у себя в магазине а также в магазине у Ярош и Мининой Т. совместно с ними оформляла бестоварные накладные, перечисленные в обвинительном заключении, а также отпускала Ярош, Мининой Т. и получала от них товары без оформления накладных. При передаче магазина продмаг №2 в январе 1978 года у нее была выявлена недостача в сумме 40601 руб. 55 коп. из которых 1900 руб. есть результат растраты вверенных ей товарно-материальных ценностей и денежных средств из продмага №2, остальная сумма недостачи возникла путем злоупотребления служебным положением. Она не согласна с суммой иска в 40601 руб. 55 коп. поскольку при составлении бестоварных накладных совместно с Ярош и Мининой Т. получалась разница, которую Ярош и Минина Т. ей не возместили.

Ярош, допрошенная в судебном заседании виновной себя признала полностью и пояснила, что действительно выявленная у нее недостача в сумме 5273 руб. 30 коп. образовалась в результате присвоения ею продуктов питания и денег в сумме 800 руб. из магазина. Она составляла совместно с Мининой Г. и Мининой Т. бестоварные накладные с целью сокрытия недостачи в своем магазине и в магазине у Мининой Г. и Мининой Т., а также отпускала товары без оформления накладных, злоупотребляя своим служебным положением.

Подсудимая Минина Тамара Н. в судебном заседании виновной себя признала полностью и пояснила, что с декабря 1976 года по январь 1978 года с целью сокрытия недостачи в вино-водочном магазине и в продмаге № 2 у Мининой Г., составляла совместно с Мининой Галиной бестоварные накладные, получая от последней и сама отпускала товары без оформления накладных, кроме этого оформила одну бестоварную накладную с Ярош, на якобы отпущенные ею в магазин Ярош Тамары товары на сумму 1086 руб. в январе 1978 года.

Прокопьева пояснила в судебном заседании, признав виновной себя частично, что действительно в сентябре 1977 года совместно с Мининой подписала накладную №45 от 8 сентября 1977 года на сумму 4173 руб. она не знала, что эта накладная является бестоварной, поскольку заведующая магазином Минина Т. была в отпуске, а Минина Г. сказала ей, что в отношении этой накладной имеется договоренность с Мининой Т.Н. Подсудимая Минина Т. в судебном заседании подтвердила показания Прокопьевой и пояснила, что Прокопьева действительно не знала, что эта накладная бестоварная.

Прокопьева также пояснила, что действительно отпускала из магазина товары без оформления накладных и 28 ноября 1977 года когда началась инвентаризация, зная о недостаче в вино-водочном магазине совместно с Мининой Т. составила три бестоварных накладных вследствии отсутствия торгового образования и навыков, она не могла понять значения бестоварных накладных, поскольку продавцом проработала несколько месяцев.

Суд проверив и оценив материалы дела считает, что квалификация действий по ст. 92ч2 УК РСФСР Мининой Галины дана правильно, поскольку в ее действиях отсутствуют квалифицирующие признаки повторность или предварительный сговор группой лиц, поэтому суд переквалифицирует ее действия на ст. 92чI УК РСФСР так как она совершила хищение государственного имущества путем растраты вверенных ей товаро-материальных ценностей на сумму I500 рублей, доказательством того является тот факт, что в период с I975 года по I977 год семья Межогских, членом которой является Минина Галина приобрели дорогостоящие вещи как шифоньер трехстворчатый, радиола ВЭФ-2, ковер размером I,5х2 м, телевизор сервант, лодка " Казанка" лодочный мотор "Вихрь" стиральную машину "Урал", мотоцикл и другие вещи.

Квалификация действий Мининой Г...

I2.

Свидетель Мингалева пояснила, что учто при проведении комплексной инвентаризации в продмаге №2 и "товары повседневного спроса" была выявлена недостача. После инвентаризации в вино-водочном магазине также выявлена недостача.

Минина Т., Прокопьева и Минина Г. признались, что скрывали недостачи путем оформления безтоварных накладных. Данные злоупотребления были бы вскрыты ранее, однако в результате бесконтрольности со стороны директора торгового предприятия Псурцевой и бухгалтера Ячменева, который ненадлежаще проводил инвентаризацию, давало возможность подсудимым скрывать недостачи.

Свидетель Маневская пояснила, что она одолжила Мининой Тамаре из своих сбережений для погашения недостачи – 2.400 руб.

Свидетель Псурцева в суде пояснила, что отчеты материально-ответственных лиц принимал в основном Ячменев он проверял все документы и как правило всегда докладывал, что все впорядке, она подписывала отчеты и отводила их в Айкино, поскольку из продмага -2 отпускались товары во многие магазины, было трудно догадаться, что подсудимые скрывают недостачи путем оформления безтоварных накладных.

Кроме этого Межогских Т. (родная сестра подсудимой Мининой Г.) пояснила, что работая в продмаге № 2 где работала и ее мать Межогских Н. действительно они брали продукты для семьи, деньги за взятые продукты платили.

Свидетель Минин А. в суде пояснил, что он работая шофером на нефтебазе, привозил товары на машине к Ярош и отвозил товары в продмаг 2 Мининой Г. и неоднократно высказывал претензии к Ярош по поводу частых перебросок из одного магазина в другой товаров.

Свидетель Растегаева пояснила в суде, что летом I977 года она раза два видела, что товары из вино-водочного магазина через окно отпускала Захарова Нина, работающая в лесничестве, несмотря на то что Минина Т. и Прокопьева были в магазине.

Суд проверив и оценив материалы дела считает, что квалификация действий по ст. 92ч2 УК РСФСР Мининой Галины дана правильно, поскольку в ее действиях отсутствуют квалифицирующие признаки повторность или предварительный сговор группой лиц, поэтому суд переквалифицирует ее действия на ст. 92чI УК РСФСР так как она совершила хищение государственного имущества путем растраты вверенных ей товаро-материальных ценностей на сумму I500 рублей, доказательством того является тот факт, что в период с I975 года по I977 год семья Межогских, членом которой является Минина Галина приобрели дорогостоящие вещи как шифоньер трехстворчатый, радиола ВЭФ-2, ковер размером I,5х2 м, телевизор сервант, лодка " Казанка" лодочный мотор "Вихрь" стиральную машину "Урал", мотоцикл и другие вещи.

Квалификация действий Мининой Г. по ст.ст. I70ч2 и I75 УК РСФСР является правильной поскольку Минина Г. злоупотребляя своим служебным положением вопреки интересам службы, из корыстных побуждений и личной заинтересованности, путем сокрытия недостачи, причинила государственным интересам а именно Усть-Вымскому району тяжкие последствия, т.е. ущерб на сумму 22.505 руб. кроме этого совершила должностный подлог в корыстных целях с целью сокрытия недостачи в своем магазине: а также в вино-водочном и в магазине " Товары повседневного спроса" путем оформления и вложения документов- безтоварных накладных и приложения их к своим отчетам при инвентаризации.

Квалификация действий Ярош Т.А. по ст.ст. 92ч3, I70ч2 и I75 УК РСФСР является правильной, поскольку Ярош совершила хищение государственного имущества злоупотребляя своим служебным положением, путем присвоения ею товаро-материальных ценностей и денежных средств, причи-

Court Record

Business №1-218 / 78 VERDICT

In the name of the RSFSR

Ust-Vymsky district court of the Komi ASSR composed of:

Presiding- Yu.D. Strugovshchikova Narzsedateley-Isakova M.E., Orlova V.N.

Secretary- Nesterenko A.

with the participation of the prosecutor - Plesovsky A.M. and lawyer- Minin V.P.

Considered in open court in the village of Zheshart, August 22, 1978 the case of the charges:

MININA GALINA EVGENYEVNA * born 7th June 1954, in the village of Zheshart of the Ust-Vymsky region of the Komi ASSR, Komi, w/w, secondary special education, married, worker at Zheshart Plywood Mill, living in the village of Zheshart. ul.Pervomayskaya 21. Previously not convicted of a crime under Article 92 Part 2, 170 Part 2 and 175 of the Criminal Code of the RSFSR

YAROSH TAMARA ALEXANDROVNI, born January 21st, 1941in Sitkovo of the Veliko-Ustyugsky district of the Vologda region, Russian, b/n, 7 years' education, married, dependents are three young children, working in the Kazluk branch of the Gamsky State Farm, living in the village of ZarucheynyUst-Vymsky region of the Komi ASSR, not previously convicted, in a crime under Art. Art. 92. P3, 170, Part 2 and 175 of the Criminal Code of the RSFSR

MININA TAMARA NIKOLAEVNY, born August 11th, 1953 in the village of Zheshart, Ust-Vymsky district of the Komi ASSR, Komi, b/n., secondary education, unmarried, working at the Zheshart timber-handling base, living in the village of Zheshart, st. Central 11, no previous convictions, in a crime under Art. 170 p.2 and 175 of the Criminal Code of the RSFSR

PROKOPYEVA MARIA NIKOLAEVNA, born on March 22, 1956, from the village of Zheshart, Ust-Vymsky region of the Komi ASSR, Komi, b / n, secondary education, married, dependent on one minor child working at the Zheshart timber-handling base, living in the village. Zheshart, st. Central 8, not previously convicted, in a crime under Art. 172 of the Criminal Code of the RSFSR

YACHMENEV LEONID NIKOLAEVICH, March 3, 1942, born in the village of Zheshart, Ust-Vymsky region of the Komi ASSR, Komi, member CPSU, secondary special education, single, disabled of the 3rd group, temporarily not working due to illness, residing in the village. Zheshart, st. Central 116, not previously convicted, in a crime under Art. 172 of the Criminal Code of the RSFSR, court

INSTALLED:

Minina G.E., Yarosh T., Minin T, Prokopyeva and Yachmenev committed a crime under the following circumstances:

Minina G., working as the head of grocery store No. 2 of the Zheshart trade enterprise of Ust-Vymsky consumer union, located in the village of Zheshart, from January 1976 to December 1977, systematically plundered the goods and material assets entrusted to her and money by embezzlement.

ten.

documents on income and expenditure.

Using this, the heads of the Prodmag stores "Consumer Goods" Minina G and "Wine and Vodka" Yarosh TA, Minina TN,. made out invoices for goods allegedly dispensed to another store - and also delivered goods without invoices and thus concealed the lack of material values, all of them here due to the theft of goods and money and the abuse of official position.

In this way, when conducting the inventory, Yachmenev was hiding shortages, which caused significant harm to Ust-Vymsky to the amount of 22.505 rubles.

Galina Minina, questioned at the court hearing, pleaded guilty and explained that she had really worked as the head of food store No. 2 from January 1976 to December 1977 to systematically conceal the shortage in her shop and that also in the store of Yarosh and Minina T.N. she had, with them, processed the non-consignment invoices listed in the indictment, and also released goods to Yarosh and Minina T.N., and received goods from them without invoices. When auditing the store Prodmag number 2 in January 1978, she had a shortage to the amount of 4.601 rubles 55 kopecks. of which 1500 rub. was as a result of the waste of the goods and materials entrusted to them, the remainder of the shortage arose through the abuse of official position. She does not agree with the amount of the claim being 4601 rubles. 55 kopecks; because in the preparation of non-repayable invoices together with Yarosh and Minina T.N., she was not reimbursed for the difference that Yarosh and Minina T.N. demanded of her.

Yarosh, questioned at the court hearing, pleaded fully guilty and explained that the shortage in the amount of 5273 rubles that she had then identified as 30 kopecks was formed as a result of the appropriation of food and money to the amount of 800 rubles. from the shop. She compiled, together with Minina G., and Minina T., non-commodity invoices in order to conceal the shortage in her shop and in the shop at Minina G., and Minina T.N., as well as selling goods without issuing invoices by abusing her official position.

The defendant Minina Tamara N., pleaded guilty in full and explained that from December 1976 to January 1978 in order to conceal the shortage in the wine-vodka shop, and in the shop number 2 in Minina G., together with Minina Galina she had fabricated invoices, and sold goods without invoices. In addition, she issued one non-compliant invoice to Yarosh for goods she allegedly sent to Tamara Yarosh's shop worth 1086 rubles. in January 1978.

Prokopyeva explained at the court hearing that she was partly guilty that in September 1977 she and Minina signed invoice no. 45 dated September 7, 1977 to the amount of 4,173 rubles, but that she did not know that this invoice was worthless. Since the shop manager

Minina T.N., was on leave, and Minina G., told her that there was an agreement with this Minina T.N., Defendant Minina T., confirmed the testimony of Prokopyeva at the court hearing and explained that Prokopyeva really didn't know about that consignment note.

Prokop'eva also explained that she had released goods from the store without invoices and on November 28, 1977 when the inventory started knowing about the shortage in the winery store together with Minina T., they made up three best invoices due to the lack of trade education and skills, she could not understand the value of non-compliant invoices, "because the seller has only worked several months."

12.

Witness Mingaleva explained that there was a shortage when carrying out a comprehensive inventory in Prodmag No. 2 "consumer goods". After an inventory, the liquor store also revealed a shortage.

Minin T,; Prokopyeva and Minin G., admitted that they hid shortages by issuing non-invoices. These abuses would have been revealed earlier, but as a result of the lack of control on the part of the director of the commercial enterprise Psurtseva and the accountant Yachmenev, who did not properly conduct the inventory, it gave the defendants the opportunity to hide the shortages.

The witness Manyevskaya explained that she had lent Minina Tamara from her savings to pay back the shortfall - 2300 rubles.

The witness Psurtseva in court explained that the reports of materially responsible persons were received mainly by Yachmenev, he checked all the documents and, as a rule, always reported that everything was in order, she signed the reports and brought them to Aikino. Since prodmag № 2 sold the goods on to many stores it was difficult to guess that the defendants hid the shortages by processing the goods without invoices.

In addition, Mezhogskikh T.Y., (the sister of the defendant Minina G) explained that she worked in Prodmag number 2 and that she and NN Mezhogsky's mother had taken food for the family, and paid for the food they took.

The witness A.A. Minin, in court, explained that he worked as a driver at a tank farm, brought goods by car to Yarosh and drove goods to Prodmag No. 2 and Minina G., and repeatedly complained to Yarosh about frequent goods transfers from one store to another.

The witness Rastegayeva explained in court, that in the summer of 1977, she had twice seen that the goods from the wine and vodka shop through the window were dismissed by Nina Zakharova working in the back area, despite the fact that Minin. T., and Prokopyeva were in the store.

The court having checked and assessed the materials of the case: considers that the qualification of actions under Art. 92h.2 of the Criminal Code of the RSFSR by Minina Galina is not correct because there are no qualifying signs or repeated collusion in her actions by the Group of persons, therefore the court reclassifies her actions at art. 92 h. 1 of the Criminal Code of the RSFSR, as it has committed, the embezzlement of state property by spending 1,500 rubles' worth of commodities entrusted to her, which is proved by the fact that in the period from 1975 to 1977 the Mezhogi family of which Minina Galina is a member acquired expensive items like a three-winged Kak wardrobe, a VEF-2 radio, a carpet 1.5x2m in size, a TV, a sideboard, a Kazanka motorboat, a Whirlwind washing machine, a Ural No.3 motorcycle and other things.

Qualification action Minin G., under Art. Art. 170 ch.2 and 175 of the Criminal Code of the RSFSR is correct because Minin G., abusing her official position against the interests of the service out of mercenary motives and a lack of interest by hiding a shortage, caused state interests, namely, Ust-Vymsky district, damages to the amount of 22,505 rubles; - besides this, she committed an official forgery for mercenary purposes in order to conceal the shortage in her store, as well as in the wine-vodka shop and in the shop of "everyday goods" by issuing counterfeit documents, invoices and applying them to the shops' inventory reports.Qualification action Yarosh TA, under Art. Art. 92, p.3., 170 ch2 and 175 of the Criminal Code of the RSFSR is correct, since Yarosh committed theft of state property by abusing her official position by assigning goods and material values and money, causing

On the penultimate day of the trial, so worried was I that Galya would be imprisoned the next day, given the bias of the interrogation and the lies of her colleagues, I borrowed money from my brother Alexander... 1000 rubles to return some of the missing money. It didn't make any difference. This action had been a serious moral a dilemma for me. For me it was already clear one hundred percent that they wanted to put Galina in jail.

During the investigation and trial, I was very depressed in spirit. Like the warriors at the beginning of the 1941 war, surprised by Hitler's attack, I had been surprised by the betrayal of Galina, whom I had loved so much. She had turned out to be rather foolish and then deceived me. From that time on, my love was gone... Happiness cannot be built on lies. On such lies the foundation of the USSR under the CPSU's leadership is built... and more cynically even today's Russia stands on lies. Not a single official fulfils their rights and obligations honestly, openly… they have long learned to lie, and to circumvent laws.

I did not know what else to do. I had an idea to ask that Galina be sent to the hospital in connection with her pregnancy, but, again, I did not listen to my inner voice. My request would have been valid. For Galina it was very difficult. During pregnancy, a woman needs rest, care and calm: but instead she had a serious investigation, her father's suicide, and now…

All that was left now was the judgement and sentencing. Although not even that public spectacle would put an end to the miserable chain of events.

10

WHO NEEDS TV?

What's the point of handing out a prison sentence to the wife of a sacked police officer if there is no audience there to enjoy it? Fortunately for the intrigued people of Zheshart, the Judge and Plesovsky had the same thought and – flying in the face of all due legal process and precedent – the next day's sentencing was moved 35 kilometres to a handy little courtroom just a 130 metres away from the police station where I had worked. The road to the courtroom (a room that was also the village gym) was almost impassable to vehicles – more of a dirt track – and the move there for the sentencing was illegal.

Predictably, the place was packed. In those days there were only two television channels, and nothing on them was as worth watching as the sentencing of a police officer's pregnant wife.

It might as well have been a televised costume drama anyway… the other defendants all arrived carrying bags and cases containing their belongings, like a displacement scene from *Dr Zhivago*. But they knew their parts well, and the script too. The bribes and networking would ensure that they were released. And so it was.

The scene of the final day's sentencing

It was August 22, 1978, three days after we had been married for a year. The state guarantees care for the family, motherhood, children, and human rights. Look at what gift the state criminals have prepared for us. Galina was the only defendant who received an immediate prison sentence, and I was the only person there who would spend the rest of my life fighting the injustice.

Injustice continued to be piled upon injustice however, as my future battles involved drugging, psychiatric imprisonment, more lies and heartbreak.

As regards the others in the dock, the verdicts were as follows: Tamara Minina received three years imprisonment with forced labour, Leonid Yachmenev received two years of conditional imprisonment with a trial period of three years.

Maria Prokopyeva got one year's corrective labour at her place of work and 20% of her salary withheld. Tamara Yarosh was given six years, which was the minimum she could have served, the sanction of the article stated six to fifteen years. Galina was given four years imprisonment and was the only one taken into custody in the courtroom. She was handcuffed and led away.

Interior of the Zheshart building, showing the gym equipment and its use as a community hall.

In modern Russia, people tend to feel good when someone else feels bad. The villagers of Zheshart had enjoyed a rewarding outcome, an invigorating dose of schadenfreude. We felt bad, they felt good. Galina was guilty and a four-year prison term would start immediately.

Had they known about my wife's impending tortuous journey to the prison or our ensuing stresses it would have been the icing on the cake for them.

*

My first reaction was to obtain the court records and lodge an appeal. Within three days of a verdict being given, the presiding judge *must* write a transcript of the hearing. I had to fight to get that transcript of the trial. Judge Strugovshchikov did not forward one to me.

I went to him to request it on 14 different days. One day, when he once again refused access to the transcript of the court session, I left his office and slammed the door. I heard Strugovshchikov shout out to me that he would put me in jail for 15 days, for contempt.

Later, I received a transcript of the court recorded by secretary Nesterenko and it was then that I saw in black and white that it was written that Galina had pleaded guilty to the crime, although it was not so– Galina did not plead guilty! It was then that I also noted that my questions to Nadezhda Mezhogsky (Galya's mother) about the items they had bought between 1975 to 1977 was missing completely. I wrote notes on the transcript to describe how the exchanges had actually happened. But I never received replies. My comments were accurate, and they knew it.

Shortly after the trial, on September 13th, an article about my wife's trial appeared in the *Vperyad* newspaper. It was a whitewashed celebration of justice having been done, written by none other than Plesovsky – the friend of Judge Strugovshchikov and our former interrogator. The article was illegal – since the sentence had not yet entered into legal force. The headline said it all:

THE TRIUMPH OF JUSTICE TAKES PLACE

ЗА ХИЩЕНИЕ СОЦИАЛИСТИЧЕСКОЙ СОБСТВЕННОСТИ—К ОТВЕТУ

Бережное отношение к народному добру является конституционной обязанностью каждого гражданина нашей страны. Об этом все знают. Однако есть еще люди, которые из-за корыстных побуждений запускают руки в государственный карман, полагая, что это для них обойдется безнаказанно. Но как говорит русская пословица: «сколько веревке не виться, а...».

Так случилось и с группой расхитителей социалистического имущества в Жешартском торговом объединении. Продавцы этого торгобъединения Галина Минина, Тамара Ярош, Мария Прокопьева, Тамара Минина, воспользовавшись халатным отношением к своим обязанностям бухгалтера торгобъединения Леонида Ячменева, организовали преступную группу и систематически совершали хищение товаро-материальных ценностей. Таким образом с января 1976 года по декабрь 1977 года ими было расхищено материальных ценностей и нанесен Усть-Вымскому райпо ущерб в сумме 22505 рублей.

Г. Минина, Т. Ярош, Т. Минина знали, что у них в магазинах недостача материальных ценностей, поэтому перед каждой плановой ревизией с целью покрытия недостачи оформляли друг другу бестоварные накладные, а также отпускали товары без оформления накладных. При проведении ревизии в одном магазине создавалось впечатление, что там все нормально — недостачи нет. Не обнаруживалась недостача и в других магазинах. И только одновременное проведение ревизий во всех магазинах позволило выявить крупные недостачи.

Несколько дней длилось судебное заседание Усть-Вымского райнарсуда, на котором рассматривалось уголовное дело по хищению социалистической собственности и злоупотреблению служебным положением группой работников Жешартского торгобъединения.

В суде выяснилось не только то, каким образом было совершено преступление, но и вскрыты причины и условия, способствовавшие его совершению; выяснилось, почему Галина Минина, Тамара Ярош, Тамара Минина, Мария Прокопьева и Леонид Ячменев оказались на скамье подсудимых.

По работе все они характеризованы положительно, выполняли общественную работу. Но работники Усть-Вымского райпо под впечатлением внешнего благополучия в магазинах Жешартского торгобъединения не замечали то обстоятельство, что между этими магазинами наблюдалось постоянное движение товаров, при том в большом количестве, в частности, винно-водочных изделий. Торговала ими и продавец Галина Минина в магазине № 2, хотя здесь это запрещено. Г. Минина за это была привлечена к административной ответственности, но и это работникам райпо не послужило поводом для более глубокой проверки работы магазина.

Нарушений со стороны этих работников прилавка было много: они брали деньги из кассы для собственных нужд, отпускали товары в долг, допускали прочие нарушения. Все это оставалось незамеченным.

Какое же моральное лицо этих людей? Во время работы и групповой сделки все они между собой жили дружно, ходили друг к другу в гости, вместе проводили свободное время. На суде выявилось их истинное лицо — лицо мелких дельцов: они спорили, валили вину друг на друга, выясняли, кто кому сколько должен, играли тысячами рублей государственных средств, как своими.

На суде каждая пыталась уйти от заслуженного наказания. Но хищение государственного и общественного имущества является опасным посягательством на социалистическую собственность, и лица, виновные в совершении таких преступлений, сурово караются законом. Народным судом Усть-Вымского района Галина Минина, Тамара Ярош, Тамара Минина осуждены к различным срокам лишения свободы; Мария Прокопьева и Леонид Ячменев также осуждены и будут отбывать наказание за совершенное преступление.

За хищение социалистической собственности районным народным судом к лишению свободы осуждена и бывшая заведующая детскими садиками № 1 и № 3 поселка Жешарт А. Г. Рамхина. Она также, злоупотребляя своим служебным положением, оформляла фиктивные накладные на «выполнение» различных работ, исполнителями указывала лиц, которые даже не знали об этом, а деньги получала сама. Таким путем ею было присвоено 1526 рублей. Как я уже отметил, она понесла заслуженное наказание.

А. ПЛЕСОВСКИЙ,
помощник прокурора района, юрист второго класса.

Plesovsky's article in the Vperyod newspaper

The headline was taken from a Russian proverb[7]. The original cutting is reproduced opposite. For a translation and further comment, you will need to wait a couple of chapters.

---

[7] For more information on this proverb see: http://chtooznachaet.ru/skolko-veryovochke-ne-vitsya.html

11

VLADIMIR

Between the end of the trial and mid-October, Galya was kept in the city of Sosnogorsk, not far from the city of Ukhta, where those waiting for their sentences to enter into legal force were kept.

On October 13th, the cassation court accepted my request for an immediate appeal. Galina had also filed a complaint. None of the others who were tried appealed. By the end of September, for ₽400, I had found myself a lawyer in Arkady Davydavich Shchegal. I explained everything to him and told him which criminal court Galina and I were under. I later found out that it was ₽400 I needn't have parted with as I did not have my wife's power of attorney and therefore no legal right to hire anybody. Moreover, the court made sure that he was unable to participate.

After five minutes of the cassation court retiring to deliberate, my appeal was rejected (a cassation court examines only the legalities of the sentencing, not the actual trial) and Shchegal, just before the hearing, appeared to hint that it was always going to be so, when he confided to me that the presiding judge, Molodtsov, knew very little about the case. This is what I have found out about Judge Molodtsov since.

He was born Vasily Alexandrovich in 1923 in a small village which was to become part of Syktyvkar. Although in 1940 he entered the Komi Teaching Institute to study Russian language and literature, the war changed his course – as it did for so many – and he was mobilised into the army.

He fought on the Leningrad Front (like Yevgeny) after graduating from military engineering school, commanded his own platoon, and was wounded three times. The third injury resulted in a disability. He was awarded twice for his war efforts: once with the *Order of The Patriotic War*, and again with the *Red Star* 'for the defence of Leningrad'. Straight after the war, in the autumn of 1945, Molodtsov entered the Leningrad Law School from which he graduated in 1952 *in absentia*.

From his native Syktyvkar he worked as a People's Judge, a Member of the Supreme Court, Deputy Minister for Justice and Deputy Chairman, as he was in

1978. He served as Chief Justice of the Supreme Court for eleven years, longer than his predecessors. He retired in 1984 after 34 years as a judge and died in 2004 aged 82.

It's a shame he didn't pay more attention to the case notes; his credentials were good! But he was two-faced. He was a soldier, fought hard, but then analyses an unfair trial and recognises the sentence as legitimate. In Russia there is a saying, "if you want to know what kind of a person someone is, make him a boss." Power changes people and shows their true face.

As regards Shchegal, I tried to find him to bring him to justice for misleading me into hiring him. He knew, first, that he could not stand in court as a 'representative' because he had been hired my me, and, second, he knew that I had no power to hire him legally anyway. In effect he stole the ₽400, as I made clear later to the police. The police looked for him for a long time, but not even improvements in new technologies could track him down. In the end they gave up due to lack of evidence, so he was never found.

It was after the cassation court approved the guilty verdict that depression really hit me with its full force. The only thing I could see to do was to complain, complain and complain.

I pointed out that Judge Strugovshchikov was a forger, a liar and a criminal. I wrote again and again, I had nothing to lose.

I pointed out the falsification of the confession – which was obvious since it was expressed in such legal terms. Galina would not have spoken thus.

I exposed how she had been criminally detained, and that Tamara Minina, who had a shortfall of ₽12,000 had bribed Komlev, who had gone on to share the bribe with Plesovsky and Strugovshchikov.

Did no one notice that nowhere in the court records had Minina been asked where the money had gone?

I described the pain and suicide of Yevgeny Mezhogsky, a patriot of the Great War.

I even offered to indicate to them the exact date that the money was embezzled! They had had the investigation notes and *Prodmag* paperwork before them the whole time but had been suspiciously incapable of making obvious connections.

I gave them the comparison I gave you my reader, between the soviet court and the Nazi trial of Dimitrov; that it was only a Russian judge at the height of communist power in 1978 that was able to slander and write down a confession instead of a pregnant woman's genuine protestations of denial.

After two and a half months of receiving these letters of complaint, on December 2nd, Strugovshchikov postponed Galya's sentence for one year, with the idea that a new-born should be with his mother until the age of one. I'm pretty sure it was because he thought I would end up killing him!

(Although it worked in our favour, I still need to mention that even the postponement was illegal. For a postponement to be granted it needs to be discussed at the original trial and statements need to be taken. So, even in this 'courtesy', or moment of self-protection, Judge Strugovshchikov was bending the law. Remember that dyshlo?)

I took a twelve-hour train journey to Golovino in the Vladimir region, after wiring ahead, to collect Galya on the very evening that I had received the telegram detailing the court's decision to postpone her sentence.

In Golovino, the prison officers were all of them incredulous. Never before had a prisoner been released, and there were in that prison one hundred pregnant women! They asked who Galina's lawyer was! No lawyer – just a husband who'd probably made the judge fear for his life with his constant stream of complaints.

There is one particular incident in all of this that never fails to elicit tears from me. I know that the words in front of me will blur as I write this. Galina told me that on her long train journey from the courtroom to the prison, she was not allowed a drink of fresh water.

The water in the prison car was stale and dirty, as the tank was never flushed out or cleaned. Just a sniff of the water produced a gagging reflex. Her requests for just a sip of fresh water were denied. She told me how her thirst was excruciating; how she worried about our baby.

A group of prisoners in the same carriage but in separate cells heard her pain and asked what was wrong. They formed a spontaneous protest group and threatened to turn the guards' carriage over unless they gave her some water. Humanity among prisoners! Thank God! Galina was offered fresh water at the next stop.

The very evening of her arrival back home, Galina's contractions began. (The prison officers had even asked her if she wanted to delay her return until the baby was born, so imminent was Vladimir's appearance.)

On December 3rd our son was born at home. I could write a whole book about the wonder of fatherhood, and the joy our darling Vladimir brought us – it is no doubt already clear to you from his involvement in procuring much of the evidence that I now have in front of me that we are still close. My son is a blessing. But this book is about injustice, and aside from the traumatic circumstances surrounding his birth and gestation (remember we nearly lost him twice due to the stress of Komlev's questioning), I like to think that we managed to shield Vladimir from the injustices we experienced. One word more though, about his name.

Modern Russia has one Vladimir famous above all others and yes – believe it or not – we named our son after Lenin!

Now that I know so much more about Lenin and the effects of his revolution upon our country I think that the choice of name wasn't so clever. Lenin brought so much evil to Russia. Thanks to his terrorist seizure of power, global changes occurred that led to millions of victims: brother went against brother, people became hardened and cruel, faith in God and humanity were lost. People assumed power according to the words of the proletarian hymn: "Whoever was nothing will become everything." So true, but not so ideal. Take a nothing drunkard from before the revolution, not working, just sitting there in his own vomit, and see him suddenly exulted to everything! Such were the people who wielded the newfound communist power: they became directors, officials, judges and more.

Lenin 1921. Time Life Pictures/Mansell/The LIFE Picture Collection/Getty Images in public domain

What can he teach and build for the state who has never done anything before? It was more than a shock to the system. It was terror.

Even as a lawyer, Lenin disappointed. As a lawyer, he of all people should have known that a court should be independent and fair. How independent and fair is this instruction, sent by Lenin in a phone message to the Politburo of the Central Committee of the RCP(b):

> A proposal to the Politburo of the Central Committee of the RCP(b) to bring Ungern to court. I advise you to pay more attention to this case, to achieve verification of the credibility of the charges and, if the proof is complete, which, apparently cannot be doubted, then arrange a public court, hold it with maximum speed, and shoot.

Accordingly, Ungern, a monarchist who fought against the Bolsheviks (and is now immortalised as a villain in the computer game 'Iron Storm', and as an often-heroic character in many European novels and short stories) was granted a six-hour show trial and then executed.

Never mind. Now the name Vladimir conjures up for me not the small, sharp-featured, behatted and moustachioed face of the soviet father who is enshrined in print and stone across the ex-communist bloc, but rather the gentle and beloved image of my only child.

12

NOT FOR THE FIRST TIME

The annals of soviet Russia are packed with stories that follow a similar pattern to my own. Avoiding the political and legal realms is no insurance against injustice, which is why Russians, a potentially warm people, are quiet and fearful. In truth, the political and legal cannot be avoided, because they infiltrate all areas of life. Every sphere of life becomes political, and when the politics are those of a corrupt federation, federal courts get involved very quickly in all issues. Here are two examples of famous Russians who, for different reasons, fell foul of the Stalinist regime. One was a scientist, the other a writer and poet.

Nikolai Vavilov – geneticist, botanist, breeder, chemist, geographer, public figure and statesman, speaker of five languages. He was sentenced to death because his approach to science was not 'Stalinist' or 'communist' in direction and he subsequently died in a soviet gulag. His life is the subject of Blackwell's 2003 novel *Hunger* and he is mentioned in *The Decemberists'* song "When the War Came", the chorus of which includes the following lyrics: *A terrible autonomy/ Has grafted onto you and me/ Our trust put in the government/ They told their lies as heaven-sent.*

Awarded the Lenin Prize for scientific research in 1926, he was prominent in the soviet government's research programmes and established his reputation based on his work on wheat, corn, and other staple crops. Traveling across the world in search of plants, he built up the world's largest seed collection in Leningrad. His driving force was to eradicate famine, and this no doubt stemmed from the fact that he'd grown up in a rural area of Moscow where crops failed regularly.

His researchers and staff showed professionalism and solidarity with the people during the siege of Leningrad by suffering extreme hunger and, in nine cases, death from starvation, rather than compromising the seed collection for food. The collection remains one of the largest and most important in the world. So, what happened to cause him to be left to die in a Siberian labour camp in 1943 aged just 55? The answer, Stalin and a protégé's treachery.

Having befriended and mentored the student Trofim Lysenko at university, Vavilov started to distance himself from Lysenko's work as it became more politically-influenced.

From that point of separation, the two men became academic and philosophical rivals in a centralised agricultural programme.

Stalin distrusted Vavilov because he had been trained in pre-revolutionary Russia and had spent over ten years traveling abroad collecting samples which made him, to Stalin's mind, likely to have been influenced by exiled 'white Russians'. The government opened a file on him in 1929.

In the late 1930s Lysenko was put in charge of Russian agriculture. Stalin preferred Lysenko because he was from a proletariat background, and because he was impressed with his success at growing and storing plants at very low temperatures. Buoyed by his success with developing crops outside of Darwinian theories, Lysenko moved further and further away from the 'bourgeois' notion of natural selection and genetics.

Vavilov, a staunch geneticist, went on a research expedition to Ukraine in 1940 where, thanks to Lysenko's plotting and on Stalin's command, he was arrested by the NKVD and subsequently sentenced to death for sabotaging Russian agriculture (in fact it was Lysenko's theories and practices that had caused the decline) and espionage. His death in 1943 was attributed to paralysis due to malnutrition, in other words starvation. Today, his genetic theories are central to biology and scientific progress. The irony that a scientist who spent his life trying to ensure that Russia would not face future famines should die from starvation is too cruel.

The second life, or fate, that I would like to present to you is that of Boris Pasternak. In the west he is most famous for his novel *Dr Zhivago*, but he had already achieved immense popularity and status in Russia due to his poetry. Stalin was among his admirers. Maybe due to 'proletarian-friendly' quotes like this: "Literature is the art of discovering something extraordinary about ordinary people".

But Pasternak's poetry became more and more critical of the revolution as he witnessed the suffering, described in his most famous novel and later made graphic in David Lean's 1965 English film. On at least one occasion, during the 'Great Purge' he was saved by Stalin personally from imprisonment (in a manner similar to Lenin's intervention with Sorokin's fate).

Stalin never could bring himself to punish Pasternak personally, maybe due to his admiration for his poetic soul or the fact that he had sought Pasternak's advice about other writers on occasion and was therefore something of a confidante. Maybe he was even to an extent in denial about the strength of Pasternak's anti-communist feeling, which became all-consuming. Despite this, as with Vavilov, a file was opened on him.

You might be thinking that much of this story shows that Stalin had a heart. No. Stalin was also a coward. He punished Pasternak in an even worse way. Through the suffering of his mistress, Olga Ivinskaya.

She was arrested in 1949 for mixing with a spy (Pasternak), sentenced to five years hard labour and, like my Galya, she was imprisoned while pregnant. The child was Pasternak's. The history books state that she miscarried while in prison. It's true. She did. But new information now shows that her miscarriage wasn't entirely unprovoked. Something else Galina and I know about. On her arrest, Pasternak was quoted as saying, "Everything is finished now. They've taken her away from me and I'll never see her again. It's like death, even worse."

Her KGB interrogator told her that she had been granted a meeting with Pasternak, whom she adored, and she was duly sent to a darkened room. She was made to climb and descend many flights of stairs until she was exhausted. Then, when the dark room was revealed, instead of seeing Pasternak she saw that she was sitting alone in a morgue. Heavily pregnant, her miscarriage followed quickly.

Even after Pasternak's death she was not spared

misery. She was rearrested with her daughter and sentenced to eight and three years respectively (though they were both released early).

In terms of how Pasternak, who survived into old age, was affected: he had to refuse the Nobel Prize in Literature, had his passport taken away, and *Dr Zhivago* had to be published in Italy and smuggled into Russia.

Both men led fascinating lives and contributed so much to both science and the arts. Both had their lives affected by fear and tragedy because they did not conform to communist rules, even though their work is recognised globally as brilliant.

In another parallel, both men have been represented in their absences. Vavilov had proposed that the seventh International Congress of Genetics be hosted in the USSR. When it was postponed by the soviet government and then relocated to Edinburgh, the Politburo refused Vavilov permission to travel and, in his honour, during the meeting an empty chair was placed on the stage to remind participants of Vavilov's 'involuntary' absence. The 1958 Nobel Prize that Pasternak was forced to refuse remained unawarded, and while stating that his non-attendance was 'voluntary' he made it clear 'between the lines' of his letter to the committee that receiving the award (which he had at first accepted) would have been a source of great personal pleasure to him.

13
PLESOVSKY'S ARTICLE

I want this chapter to be all about the article in the newspaper that followed Galina's trial. It says so much about both the character of the prosecutor who wrote it, and the target readership it was meant to appeal to. Overall though, I think the main target was his drinking companion Strugovshchikov who might have been feeling guilty about his actions and needing a bit of cheering up.

Five... six... seven... eight... Who do we appreciate? STRUGOVSHCHIKOV!

This is the article, dated September 12th, 1978, translated into English from the Russian:

FOR THE THEFT OF SOCIALIST PROPERTY – THE VERDICT

A CAREFUL ATTITUDE REGARDING the general good is the constitutional duty of every citizen of our country. Everyone knows this. However, there still exist people who, because of self-serving incentives, launch their hands into the state pocket, believing that they will not face justice. But as the Russian proverb says: even the rope that curls[8] ...

This very thing happened to a group of plunderers of socialist property in the Zheshart Trade Association. Retailers in this organisation, Galina Minina, Tamara Yarosh, Maria Prokopyeva, Tamara Minina took advantage of the negligence of the trade accountant Leonid Yachmenev by organising a small criminal group and systematically committing fraud. In this way, from January 1976 to December 1977, they stole material assets and caused damage to the Ust-Vymsky economy to the amount of 22,505 roubles.

G. Minin, T. Yarosh, T. Minin knew that there were shortfalls in the material values in their stores so each had planned their action, making out invoices to each other as well as releasing the goods without invoices. When an audit was performed in a store, the impression was that everything was as it should be - there was no shortfall, and no shortfalls in other stores either.

---

[8] 'Even the rope that curls has an end." It is futile to twist things.

Only when the audits were conducted simultaneously across all the stores were we able to identify the major discrepancies.

The session of the Ust-Vymsky court lasted for several days, during which time the criminal case of the embezzlement of socialist property and abuse of official positions by a group of employees of the Zheshart Prodmag chain was heard. The court ascertained not only the ways in which the crimes were committed, but also the reasons and conditions that contributed to their occurrence. It resulted in Galina Minina, Tamara Yarosh, Tamara Minina, Maria Prokopyeva and Leonid Yachmenev being placed in the dock.

According to their work, they were all characterised positively. But the workers of Ust-Vymsky, under the delusion of superficial success in the shops, did not notice the fact that there was a constant movement of goods between these shops, despite the large quantities involved, of wine and vodka products in particular. The retailed Galina Minina also sold alcohol in store no.2 even though this was illegal. Mrs Minina was held to account for this, but even that was not enough reason for the workers to look deeper into the store workings. There were many violations by these workers at the counter: they took money from the cash register for their own needs, released goods into debt, and committed other violations. It all went unnoticed.

What is the moral face of these people? During work and group dealings they lived in harmony between themselves, they visited each other in their spare time. At trial, their true faces were revealed – the faces of small businessmen: they argued, they threw the blame around, found out who dealt with whom, how much he owed, played with thousands of state roubles as if they were their own.

At trial, each tried to escape from their well-deserved punishment. But embezzlement of state and public property is a dangerous encroachment onto socialist property and the perpetrators of such crimes are severely punished by law. Galina Minina, Tamara Yarosh, Tamara Minina were sentenced to various terms of imprisonment by the People's Court of the Ust-Vymsky District. Maria Prokopyeva and Leonid Yachmenev were also convicted and will serve their sentences for the crime.

A Plesovsky. Assistant District Attorney;
Second Class Lawyer

The article itself is completely contrary to the verdict itself. It states that the crime was that of a group of persons through prior conspiracy, but this was not confirmed in the verdict. The article states that everyone was sentenced to imprisonment but only Galina and Yarosh Tamara were imprisoned. Minina, Prokopyeva, and Yachmenev received suspended sentences. Yachmenev, the main auditor, was a member of the CPSU and he was not even expelled from the party. This implies that the party itself created the conditions for fraud and embezzlement: which sat well with its policy of division and power.

Plesovsky wrote his article in the Stalinist spirit of the 'struggle against the enemies of the people', and no doubt with at least one other brand of spirit exerting its influence too.

In 2010, in my capacity as the defence lawyer and with therefore a position equal to that of Plesovsky the prosecutor, I approached the *Vperyad* newspaper with my refutation of the article and the exposure of the real crimes that were committed on September 12th, 1978. But they denied my rights and my claims. Such is the freedom of speech in a now 'democratic' Russia.

With my son Vladimir, I also filed a lawsuit against the prosecutor's office regarding the protection of honour and dignity. As a general rule, prosecutors and judges in Russia are stupid and don't even know how to lie properly, despite all the practice they get.

At the trial we faced opposition from three prosecutors, a judge and a secretary. Just listen to what nonsense the prosecutors threw out!

At first, they stated that the statute of limitations had passed. We easily dismissed this – there is no limitation on the intangible personal rights laws. But beyond that, the prosecutors said something even more stupid: that the article was from a different district and region! This nonsense was easily refuted by the article itself in which the village of Zheshart is mentioned, as well as the Ust-Vymsky court and so on!

Because losing was not in their plans, the court simply ended up ruling that we did not have the right to go to court on a notarised power of attorney. Even though I had filed a preliminary complaint with the Supreme Court of the Komi ASSR.

I wonder if, through his article, Plesovsky did actually manage to apply balm to Judge Strugovshchikov's troubled mind? The judge who, instead of writing down my wife's actual words of denial and confusion wrote down two fabricated words of confession, the judge who destroyed the testimony of an important alibi, Nadezhda, and the judge who detained Galina for no reason. The law states that bail should only be disallowed where the defendant might commit another crime or abscond. Where would a pregnant woman run to? Especially one who had committed no crime?

As a frustrating but also quite amusing aside, I also complained about my wife's treatment to a number of other soviet media outlets around the same time, in the hope that they might take up my story. I received a reply from one newspaper: *Komsomolskaya Pravda*. They replied to tell me that a newspaper could not change or cancel Galina's sentence. What a stupid answer! I knew as well as any lawyer that only a higher court could do that.

14

PSYCHIATRIC HOSPITAL NO. 15

Should I have left it at that? I know that many would still advise that I should have done so. Especially given the toll it has taken on my health and the extent to which the fight I took up also took over my life.

But this is not just a fight to clear Galina's name, or to expose particular judges and their cronies. My concern is also for Russia. Where people are still living in fear of being falsely accused and imprisoned. Perhaps you have an inkling that I might be exaggerating. I don't know how much the West is taught about the legacy of Stalin and the fear that still persists. I know that Russian people have an international reputation for deep kindness and soulfulness. No. Russian people are quiet because they are scared.

There is a documentary currently online that will show and tell you the same thing: from the perspective of a writer younger and less bitter than me. Nevertheless, he opens with a memorable line that pretty much sums it all up: "where injustice wins, but we know we are right."[8] Through the words of the curator of the Gulag Museum in Moscow, his film recounts the fairly well publicised story of a girl who had just left school for a job selling ice-cream. One day she was excited to see her friends from school, her ex-classmates. From her cart she handed each of them an ice-cream with the intention of paying at the end of the day when she returned to the warehouse. But on her return the cart was immediately sealed up and the girl was sent to the notorious Kolyma Gulag… for embezzlement.

That crime again. Embezzlement. That same sanctimonious complaint of stealing from the state. This is why I continue to fight.

And this is how my fight continued in 1979…

It was October, Vladimir was ten months old and Galina would shortly be returning to prison for her suspended four-year term of incarceration. I decided to take my concerns to the American Embassy in Moscow.

---

[8]"Kolyma – Birthplace of Our Fear"
https://www.youtube.com/watch?v=oo1WouI38rQ

I had been listening to various radio stations: '*Voice of America*', '*BBC*', '*Freedom*', *Deutsche Welle*' and others. These stations had all been banned in the USSR and were characterised to the general Russian populace as anti-Soviet, preaching freedom and democracy. Before they were banned they had been listened to widely. Galina even remembers her father listening to the BBC.

On these stations I heard the West reporting on human rights violations in the USSR, and I heard the soviet lies that followed in response.

It was around the time that I decided to visit Moscow that I heard on the radio that a group of conservatives had broken into the US embassy, asking for political asylum.

My reasons for visiting the embassy was not just with regard to Galina's miscarriage of justice – I wasn't so irrational in my anger as to think the Americans would be worried about embezzlement in *Prodmag No. 2.* I was going to mention it of course, but the main purpose of my visit was to tell them about the genocidal treatment and the disenfranchisement of the Komi people by the soviet government and the horrors of Russian justice and human rights. The problem was far greater than the focus of this memoir gives me room to explain, and I will not digress, now, as we approach the closing scenes. Suffice to say that I took with me to Moscow a portfolio crammed with documents relating to human rights violations.

I made my way by train to Moscow, travelling across Kirov. I met up with my friend Gennady. We sat in the dining car and I told him everything that had happened. I asked him to accompany me to the embassy so as not to be alone. He refused, despite the help that I had given him years before when he was taken to court by an ex-girlfriend. When I rose from the table, I spilled the salt and took it as a bad omen.

*

It felt like a dream to be in Moscow, standing in front of the American Embassy that was bestrewn with flags. The stars and stripes! It was like a scene from a movie, and I admit that despite my mental exhaustion I did have a thrill of excitement as I contemplated the conversations I intended to have. A dream come true, one might say, to share details about the worst violations of human rights and the most criminal judges with an office that stood for democracy and freedom. I remember that, not far from the entrance, was a *Zhiguli* car, stranded without its wheels. The date was October 13th, 1979.

Outside the entrance to the embassy was a booth in

which there were soviet policemen who guarded the outside and American officers who guarded the inside. I entered the booth and was immediately stopped and questioned. A police officer told me that first I needed to be invited by the Embassy and given a pass.

Maybe they suspected that I was trouble with my portfolio of papers under my arm. They grabbed me and at once three of them started to drag me towards a police car. I resisted very strongly, and it took them a long while to get me there. I shouted loudly and asked passers-by for help.

I was taken to the Moscow police department. I don't know why. They spoke to me a little bit, just a little bit.

A car came from the psychiatric hospital and two nurses now took me. As we drove past a kiosk selling newspapers, one of the nurses, laughing, taunted me: "You want the truth? Well, there's the truth in the kiosk, selling for three kopeks."

Psychiatric hospital no. 15 in the 3rd ward (Kashirskoye Metro Station) was where I then found myself. They examined me and sent me to the showers, then they tied me down to a bed and injected my backside.

At first, the pain from it was slight, but it intensified gradually. The hellish pain of feeling that your spine was being twisted backwards. It was impossible to endure as it culminated in the feeling that every muscle in my body was being unnaturally twisted. I began to scream, just as an outlet for the pain, and was promptly given two more injections; this time in my arm. Shortly afterwards the pain did start to subside.

My guess was that I had first been injected with some kind of nerve agent or muscle paralysis agent, as an attempt at intimidation. Under Stalin, people were shot with a firearm. Under Breshnev, people were shot with chemicals in a mental hospital.

The next day there was some reprieve from the controlling drugs, and I was visited by two psychiatrists. I remember the man's face being covered entirely by a serious case of acne, while the woman was very beautiful and turned out to be head of the department. It occurred to me how wrong it was that doctors took the Hippocratic oath to look after the sick but instead, in return for the best cars, the best salaries, wads of vacation vouchers they followed authority instructions to make the healthy ill.

In the ward where I lay there was always an orderly who would be watching over everyone. She would give me my pills then examine my mouth to check that I had swallowed them. And deception in those circumstances was impossible.

There were also voluntary workers among the long-term patients there. They would spend the working day sealing adhesive envelopes. I wrote a short letter to Galina, telling her that I was still in Moscow but in a ward for the mentally ill and that she should come to get me. When I went to the toilet, I asked a woman visitor to post the letter for me. She obviously did so, and I thank her for that mercy. Galina arrived a few days later with her youngest brother Valera. I lay there in that ward, taking unnamed pills, for twenty long days. It was a completely mysterious episode over which I had no control or the slightest say.

However, some light was shed on the situation when, upon my transfer by train from Moscow to Syktyvkar psychiatric hospital, via a police station, I caught sight of documents that outlined my diagnosis: paranoid schizophrenia.

They continued to give me the same pills at Syktyvkar, but they did not check mouths with the same degree of dedication. I didn't swallow a single one during my two-week stay.

At least I now had presence of mind. In a newspaper I saw a report about an amnesty being extended to all women with minors. This was in connection with it being the *International Year of the Child*. Tamara Yarosh also benefited under the same amnesty. I went straight to the psychiatrist and explained that since Galina need no longer face prison because of the amnesty that was in the process of being granted, I no longer had any reason to fight the system. They explained that they needed to keep me in 'quarantine' for one week – I imagine they were seeking advice as to what they should do with me – and then… I was finally discharged.

Two weeks later Judge Strugovshchikov called us both in and gave us the papers relating to the amnesty. His hatred of us was written all over his face!

I suppose that really that last short paragraph was the *grand finale, the dénouement*. The end of my adventures.

I wanted to forget myself and get away from these thoughts, it was very hard for me. I put all my energies over the next twelve months into building us a new family home from scratch. I pretty much built that house alone. After a year of construction, we were already living in it. But I had no moral or physical strength left. I did not even have the power or resolve to hammer in one more nail.

I am still very tired.

As Vladimir grew up little by little he would cry far more when I left the house than when Galina left to go to work. Galina became convinced that I would leave her. Scandals around her fidelity started, such was her love for me. We decided that it would be better for us to move. We sold the house and she left me.

Sometime later, Galina returned to me and said she wanted to start a family again. She said she had realised that I was calm and competent, had a sensible head on my shoulders and didn't drink. I wonder who she had mixed with while she was away.

Ever since, there has not been a day that's gone past in which I haven't thought about the case, about Strugovshchikov the criminal judge, and the slander of my wife. It was always my aim to quash the sentence, but in the USSR such a thing is impossible, as I learnt the hard way. Every year I went to human rights defence lawyers in Moscow, but I always received the same response. Through that I understood that they were all of them recruited by the KGB. They received money from the KGB and did not care for the falsely convicted.

Once, in Moscow, I wanted to get in touch with American diplomats and journalists. The embassy cars displayed the phone numbers… and so I called. My own voice was met with a beautifully concerned female voice that asked me what I was worried about. At that moment of her asking I saw a light come on in the phone booth. I hung up and ran. It was a sign that we were being listened to by the authorities.

Perestroika began. In the 'new' political climate I wrote several more complaints, but the answers were old. "The sentence is lawful and justified, there are no grounds for cancellation or amendment."

Ten years later and I was in Russia again. The USSR had fallen but its methods and practices were going nowhere… and happiness will never be built from a lie.

EPILOGUE

Such is my life and fate. This is the fate of the country as a whole.

In Russia, people from ancient times came up with different proverbs, based on life experience. One of these proverbs says, "you cannot build happiness on a lie." This proverb is indeed true.

Look, Galina married me by tricking me into hiding her problems. That's no way to live. You have to be honest in a relationship, you cannot cheat. You have to have trust and respect. This is what her deception has led to, so much pain, so much suffering, and so many sacrifices. That's all I can blame her for.

The main lie is the deception upon which modern Russia, c.1917, is built. After the court case, I began to read "between the lines" of what we were told by the press and through the history of the USSR as it is taught in school.

In 1917 there was *not* a revolution, but a terrorist seizure of power. Criminals came to power, parasites who perverted everything – faith, thinking, lifestyles. The country plunged into terror and lies. The communists said they would give freedom and land to the peasants, and the result was one big concentration camp with millions of innocent victims. The whole country is built by prisoners. How many people died and suffered innocently? Unknown numbers, and it's disgusting. I'd refer you back to a previous chapter about Vavilov and Pasternak. There are so many other examples though.

Then I found all the information about the friendship between Hitler, Stalin and Molotov – *rebentropa*. Two dictators wanted to take over the world, but Hitler was smarter. Few people in Russia know about the friendship between Hitler and Stalin and that Stalin was involved in the occupation with Hitler and that the war began on September 1, 1939. Even now, Russia is still falsifying history and trying to deny the friendship of Hitler and Stalin.

In Russia, there is a proverb "better bitter truth than a sweet lie." But this sweet lie has claimed millions of lives and will take more in the future. Upon these misconceptions, millions of people have suffered. It's why Russia is so disliked in Europe: they all know about the occupation of the USSR. In Russia, people do not understand and do not want to understand. In Russia, we are encouraged to blame the West for all of our troubles. Is the West arranging terror in Russia? Is it the West taking bribes and creating arbitrariness in Russia? Was it a judge from the West that sentenced Galina?

Even when there was an accident at the Chernobyl nuclear power plant, the USSR stubbornly kept its silence and tried to hide the tragedy – exposing its people to huge dangers. At that time, I listened to Western radio stations which the USSR tried to block and from them I heard that the USSR was radioactive with the pollution.

When *Perestroika* began, and in 1991 the communist system collapsed, I tried again to overturn Galina's verdict, but only the name of the country was changed, its essence remained and still remains the same.

Nothing changes, the totalitarian regime is still the same, people are still disenfranchised, there are no human rights and freedoms, there is no independent media, the press is completely false and corrupt, and justice is a concept of which we can only dream.

The exiled Russian poet Lermontov wrote in 1841:

Goodbye, unwashed Russia,
Land of slaves, land of masters,
And you, blue uniforms,
And you, their loyal people.

Since his pain then nothing has changed, except that it has become even worse…

A few years ago, I created a petition for clearing the name of the war participant Yevgeny Mezhogsky and for the revision of the verdict against Galina. I walked through the city of Syktyvkar and stopped people and told my story asking people to sign a petition on the Internet.

I stopped about 20 people, all of them said that they would sign the petition, but a day later, weeks later, not a single name had been added. But I was more struck by another side to this episode: I stopped and asked a 25-year-old man to sign the petition supporting Galina's dad, Yevgeny. He refused, saying that he had never sent Russian soldiers anywhere personally, and that he didn't care about any of them, including Yevgeny. I was shocked at first, and then realised he was honest with me and spoke directly – unlike those 20 hypocritical people who said they would sign.

So, there you have it. Such is the nature of the modern Russian soul. With its deceit, meanness and lies.

There are good people, but they are few.

Take care in your life, don't do anything stupid. Life is given once, so live it with dignity and honesty, trusting in your loved ones.

Do good and possibly good will return to you.

Don't be cruel, as it causes pain and the pain causes scars. Like a knife in the back.

All trouble in Russia is rooted in the criminal court. A person in front of such a court is helpless and can do nothing, they face a solid wall. I don't understand Komlev, Strugovshchikov, Plesovsky and other such judges and prosecutors... How can I? My mind does not grasp them to this day. So many lives have been broken by their desire for those five-minute bursts of power and personal euphoria.

The deception on the part of Judge Strugovschikov is the ingenious inventiveness Russians show in relation to non-Russians... that is why Russians are dangerous to their citizens and to the whole world. I can do nothing but consider all judges and prosecutors in the USSR and present day Russia to be *the main evil*: terrorists and fascists. And all the judges, with the help of all the moronic, hate-filled prosecutors deliberately destroyed the USSR - and yet this is falsified in our history. They destroyed the USSR, Americans, Yeltsin, Gorbachev... destroyed all.

They have been destroying Russia since 1917 when they came to power "whoever was nothing he will become everything."

The only dream I still have is that the criminal sentencing of my wife by Judge Strugovschikov, the sentencing that meant nothing to him but which condemned my family to sadness, be cancelled. Wiped from local and personal history… Ah, but I do have another dream: as a child I was cold and slept very badly at night, and now I so want to sleep calmly, eyes shut tightly, right the way through to morning.

Printed in Great Britain
by Amazon